NOTICE BOOK
EAREY
ⴱ ⵍ ⵣ

KBS
EDOM
Amalekite
Mitanni
The Philistines
Elam
Sumer and Akkad
Sumero-Akkadian Word

From Cradle Civilization to John Revelation: 9:14

Book -1-

SHORT HISTORY
of the first of the Civilization
of Mankind on Earth
By: Joseph E. Bahri Bek
ⴱ ⵍ ⵣ
& Some Arbic words.
وقيد عربيد

Book -2-   First Religion to Exist
In Arbic
By Joseph E. Bahri Bek
من قبل عزيزي

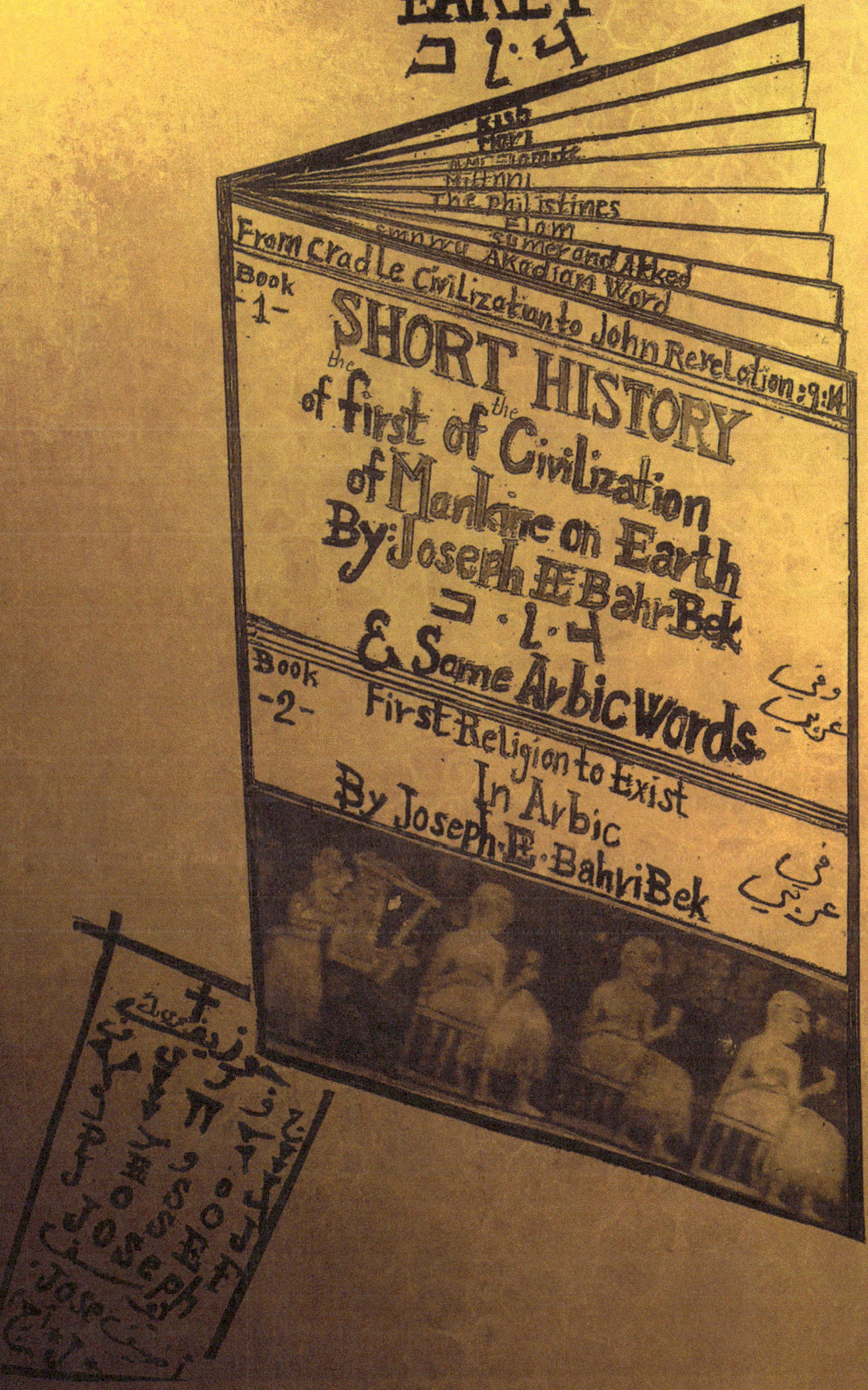

NOTICE BOOK
EAREY

Kish
Mari
Hurrians
The Philistines
Elam
Sumer and Akkad
Amurru Akadian Word

From Cradle Civilization to John Revelation :9:14

Book -1-

SHORT HISTORY
of the first of the Civilization
of Mankind on Earth
By: Joseph E Bahr Bek
& Some Arbic words.

Book -2-

First Religion to Exist
In Arbic
By Joseph E. Bahri Bek

ARPress
ILLUMINATING IDEAS
EMPOWERING VOICES

ARPress
45 Dan Road Suite 5
Canton MA 02021

Hotline:	1(888) 821-0229
Fax:	1(508) 545-7580

Ordering Information:

Quantity sales. Special discounts are available on quantity purchases by corporations, associations, and others. For details, contact the publisher at the address above.

Printed in the United States of America.

ISBN-13:   Softcover   979-8-89389-277-2

Library of Congress Control Number: 2024908170

INTRODUCTION

مقدمه

Hi

Hi my dear Reader this Book

《NotesBook Early Short History of the first of Civilization of Mankine on Earth 》 the first Existence of the Civilization Starting in Mesopotamia to find What they have done in their period, or Dynasty from their Art Artitechtur. And from their Writing the Low Agriculture in the Book #1 show you that all Life first began in the Mesopotamia And ALL of the Spot of the Word Also Will End the Life on plant the Earth As been Writtin in the Holy Book John Revelation in New Testament Bible- 9:14

(9:14)

And Also in this book there are Book #2 · I Wrote from the first Religions Appeared from ALL Spots on the Earth Exist from their Worshipping their own gods or Gods on their brain guide them toWards Their Ideis & Mythologically and their rutuals or faith What Ever Come in their mine What Ever Believe and Sure their fiath. Thank you My God Bless all notions on the Earth

publisher: Joseph Eshoo BahriBek

⊐*ۀ*ٮ* *J*Ɛ*B*

هلو أغزائي

هو وعزيزي القارئ هذا كتاب كتاب الملاحظات في الأولى نشوء الحضارات على سطح الأرض بدأت في وادي الرافدين وفي بقيّة أنحاء العالم نقطة بدأة أول حياة على الأرض في وادي الرافدين وستنتهي في وادي الرافدين كما دوّنت في كتاب رؤيا يوحنا المقدّس ٩:١٤ وما عملوا في عهد دولاتهم أو في عهد أو الدور من فنّهم وفنّ البناء والكتابة وقانوف والزراعة والح في هذا كتاب رقم واحد (١) يبين لك كل هذا أول حياة بدأت في وادي الرافدين ومنها في بقيّة أنحاء العالم وسوف أيضاً تنتهي الحياة في وادي الرافدين كما مذكورة ومدوّنه في كتاب رؤيا يوحنا (١٤:٩)

فبعد الجديد، وأيضاً في هذا الكتاب يوجد كتاب آخر كتاب رقم 2 حيث دوّنت ظهور ووجود أوّل أديان في بقاء أنحاء العالم على أرض حين ظهرت أوّل عبادات الله أو ألله جميعاً ما نشاء عقولهم من الخرافات وأفكار التي تنبثق من عقل وعقولهم وعبادتهم واعتقاداتهم وأيمانهم وعبادتهم يثقون بواقع شكراً والرب القطم بارك كلّ أمة على الأرض وكل أمم

من جوزيف أيشو بحري بك

⊐*ۀ*ٮ* *J*Ɛ*B*

I DO BELIEVE GOD SO MUCH AND EXIST.   J*Ɛ*B*

⊐*ۀ*ٮ*

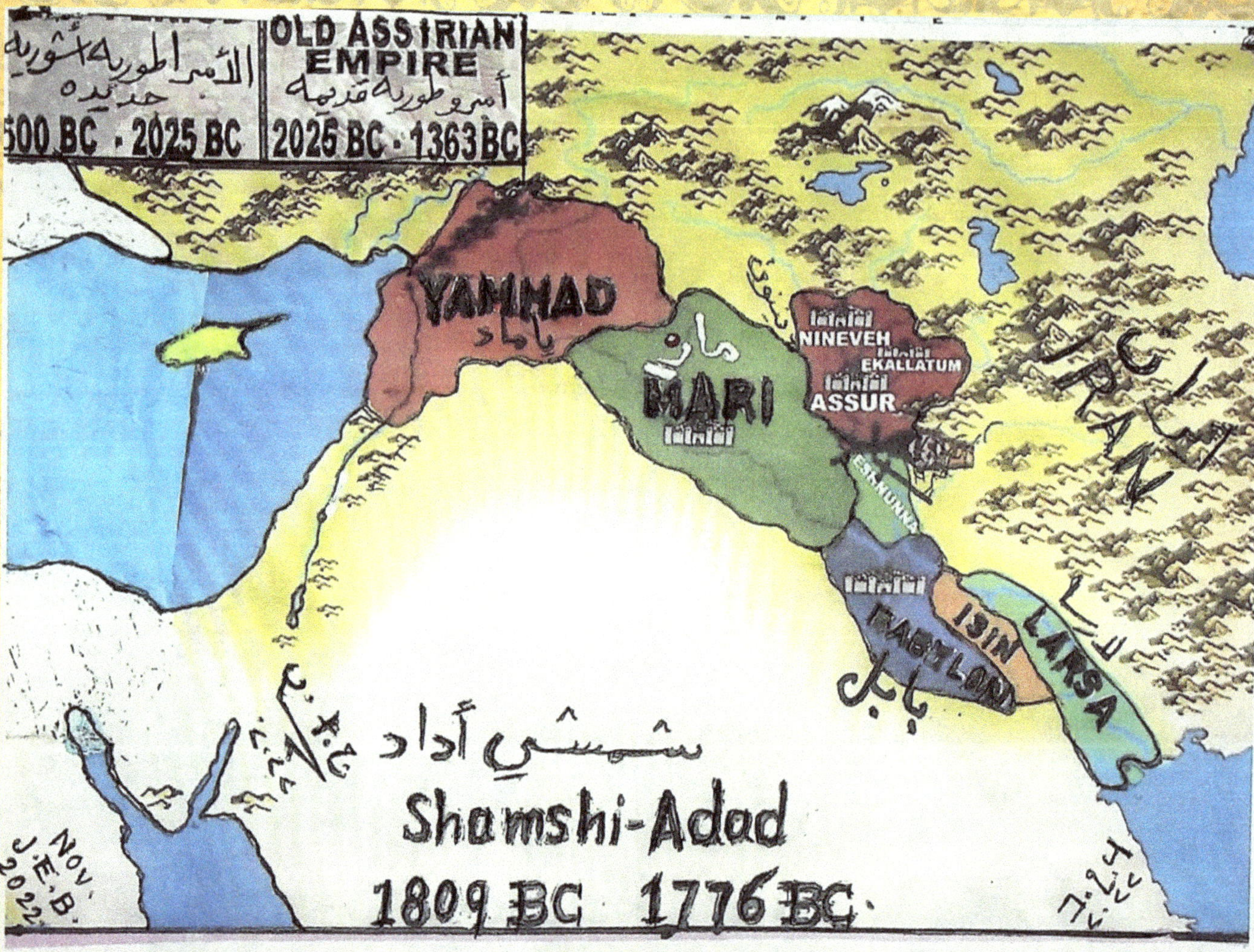
الأمبراطورية أشورية حديثة
500 BC - 2025 BC
OLD ASSIRIAN EMPIRE
أمبراطورية قديمة
2026 BC - 1363 BC
YAMHAD
يامحاد
ماري
MARI
NINEVEH
EKALLATUM
ASSUR
ESHNUNNA
BABYLON
ISIN
LARSA
بابل
IRAN
إيران
شمشي أداد
Shamshi-Adad
1809 BC 1776 BC
NOV. J.E.B. 2022

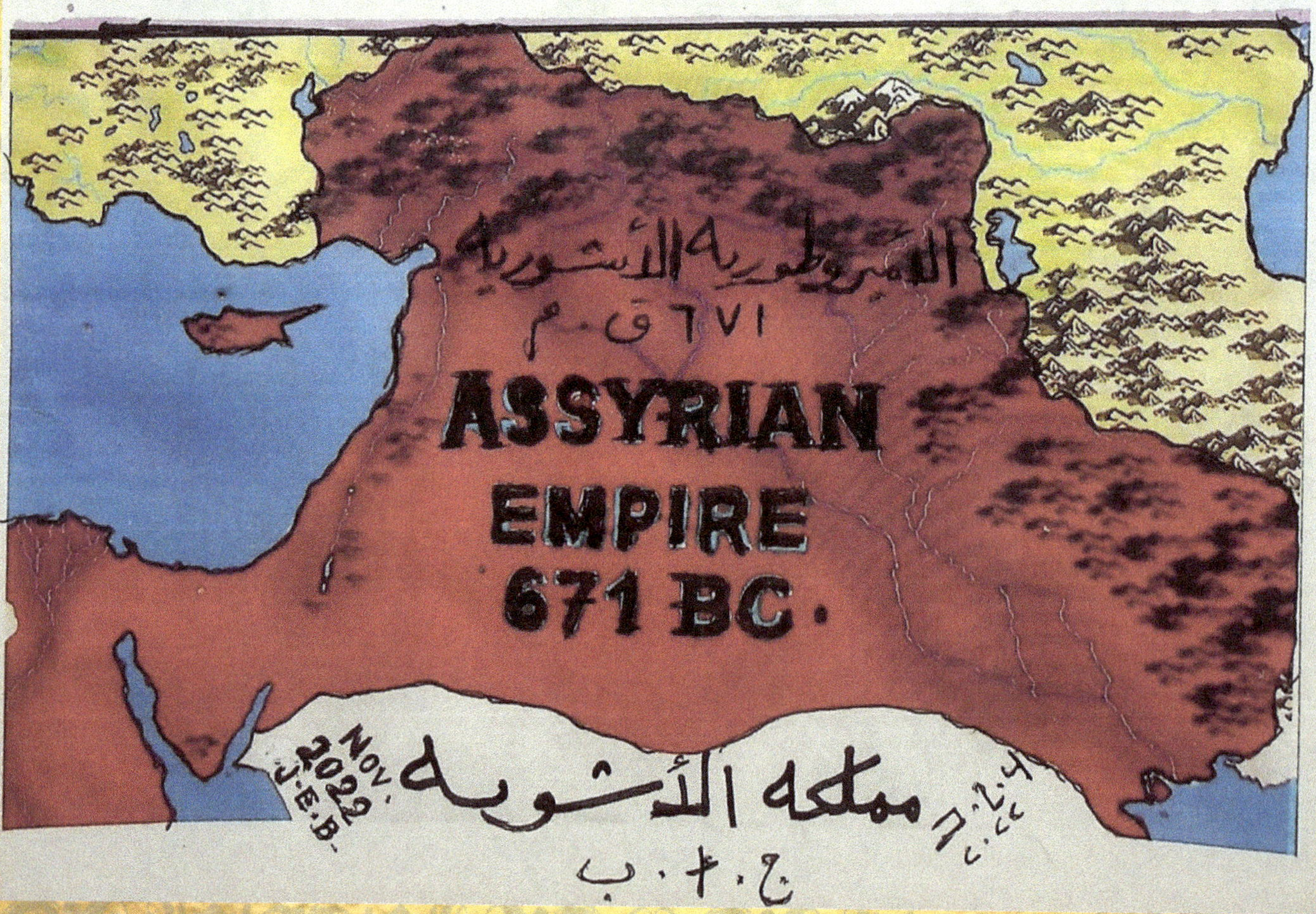
الامبراطورية الأشورية
٦٧١ ق.م
ASSYRIAN
EMPIRE
671 BC.
NOV. 2022 J.E.B.
مملكة الأشورية
ج.ع.ب

* Amurru : Akadian Word
 For Amyitie : and Also
 Mean Nest
* Sumerian : Cal : MAR TU ; Amorite

Third Dynasty of Ur

Neo- Sumrian
Ur. Nammu Empire   2112 - 2095 · B·C·
Shulgi   2094 - 2047 · B·C·
Amar- Sin   2046 - 2038 · B·C·
Shu - Sin   2037 · 2029 B·C·
Ibbi Sin   2028 - 2004 · B·C·

* kassite
kassu in Akkadian Word the name is Samatic
kalzu in kassit
Name of knssite they Come from Zaigras
Mentain North Weastram IRAN
First menti kssitc
First mention
is during of Word kaššu
* First Dynasty of Babylon 1894-1595 B.C.E.
* kassit Control of Northern Babylonia Was
 or Obally Consoliated around the year 1570 B.C.E
* By 1600 · B·C· the first Dyinsty of the SeaLand
 Controls Southern Mesopotanian · aka Sumer
* The kassit Unity Babylonia ((mor or Less
Anciant : Sumer and Akked)) onec ·

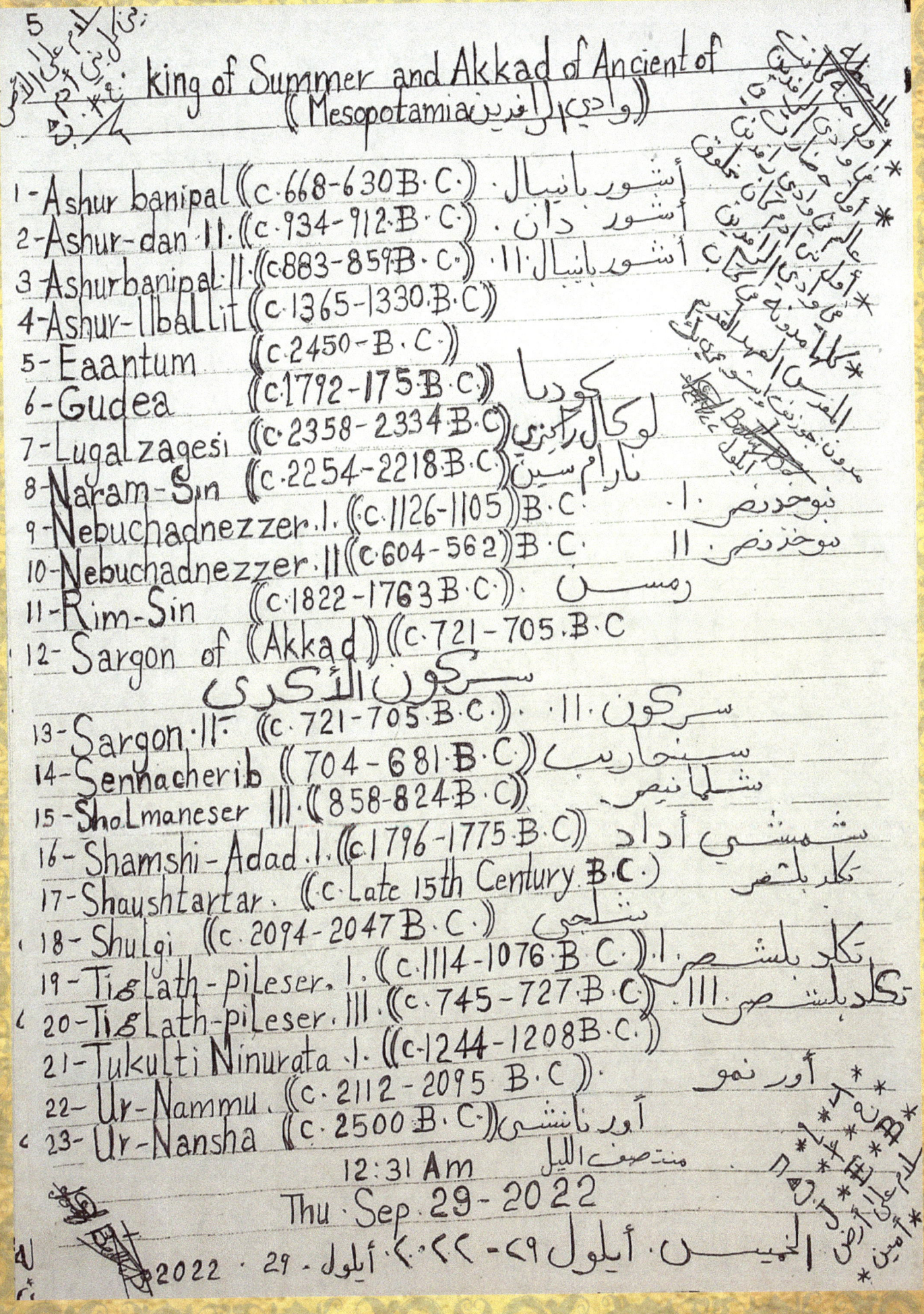

king of Summer and Akkad of Ancient of (Mesopotamia) (وادي الرافدين)

1- Ashur banipal ((c.668-630 B·C·)) أشور بانيبال
2- Ashur-dan II. ((c.934-912·B·C·)) أشور دان
3- Ashurbanipal. II ((c.883-859 B·C·)) أشور بانيبال II
4- Ashur-Uballit ((c.1365-1330·B·C·))
5- Eaantum ((c.2450-B·C·))
6- Gudea ((c.1792-175·B·C·)) كوديا
7- Lugalzagesi ((c.2358-2334 B·C)) لوكال زاكيزي
8- Naram-Sin ((c.2254-2218 B·C·)) نارام سين
9- Nebuchadnezzer.I. ((c.1126-1105)) B·C· نبوخذ نصر .I.
10- Nebuchadnezzer. II ((c.604-562)) B·C· نبوخذ نصر II
11- Rim-Sin ((c.1822-1763 B·C·)) رمسن
12- Sargon of ((Akkad)) ((c.721-705·B·C
سركون الأكدي
13- Sargon. II· ((c.721-705·B·C·)) سركون .II.
14- Sennacherib ((704-681·B·C·)) سنحاريب
15- Sholmaneser III· ((858-824 B·C·)) شلما نصر
16- Shamshi-Adad.I. ((c.1796-1775·B·C·)) شمشي أداد
17- Shaushtartar. ((c.Late 15th Century·B·C·)) شاوشتتص
18- Shulgi ((c.2094-2047·B·C·)) شلجي
19- Tiglath-Pileser.I. ((c.1114-1076 B·C·)) تكلاد بلش صر .I.
20- Tiglath-Pileser.III· ((c.745-727·B·C·)) تكلاد بلش صر III
21- Tukulti Ninurata.I. ((c.1244-1208 B·C·))
22- Ur-Nammu. ((c.2112-2095·B·C)). أور نمو
23- Ur-Nansha ((c.2500·B·C·)) أور نانشى

12:31 Am   منتصف الليل
Thu· Sep·29-2022
2022 · 29 - أيلول ؟ ٢٠٢٢ - ٢٩ - أيلول الخميس

نبذة مختصرة عن

تكمله خلف صفحه

٦٠

نبذة مختصرة عن تاريخ العراق القديم B.C .... years

من حوالي 3000 B.C سنة قبل الميلاد بلاد ما بين النهرين (Mesopotamia)

ازدهرت الحضارة في العراق القديم أو بلاد ما بين النهرين كما كانت تسمى في أطلق المعاصرين حين تكن البلاد موحده في عصر مملكة كبيره موحده وفي تلك الفتره إنشر عصر حضاره قديم كبرى كانت مجموعه من الحضارات المتفرقه يعيش هم اقدم حضارة summer

بلاد ما بين النهرين وهي في عالم كل وفي فتره بدأت تتشكل معالم حضاره ما بين النهرين مثل فنون الكتابه والزراعه والعماره والدين والأدب والطبي god

الأكدين: انتهى في عصر السلالات يقام الملك (أكدى) بتوحيد بلاد ما بين النهرين في مملكة واحده مملكة كبيره موحده حوالي 2350 year قبل الميلاد حكم Sargon B.C (Sargon) سنه 5.5 years ادخل جلال الأكدين كثيرمن الاصلاحات على نظام الملك والبلاد لكن وصل بلاد ما بين النهرين لقمة الازدهار ها Neram Sin

خلال عصر الأكدين في عهد الملك نرام سين احد ملوك خلال الأكدين كان حكم نرام سين اعظم الملوك الأكدين 100 البلاد ودوستوني على المنطقه وعرفت قبائل الجوتس الجبليه سنه وكانت تلك الفتره مظلمه في تاريخ العراق في وادي الرافدين القديم لكن ما عوض عن ذلك هو ازدهار الحضاره السومريه في جنوب العراق وبح في النهايه ملك سومري كان اسمه أوتوحيكال من هيبه الجوتس واعاده التوحيد بلاد واخذ Auto Hekal لقب ملك سومر والأكاد وبعد ذلك انتقل الملوك الى مدينه أور king Ur Namu سس ملك أور نمو ملك سلاله أور جديده تكونت تلك السلاله من 5 ملوك kings وبح ملوك

(5) في اعاده انشاء امبراطوريه واسعه مثل امبراطوريه الأكديه القديمه حكمت مناطق واسعه في الشرق الأدنى القديم العصر البابلي قديم: قبل 2000 B.C year قامت في البلاد ما بين النهرين سلاله بابليه الجديده وعرفت بالبابليين سلاله ملوك Hamurabi العادل وبح حمورابي الذي بح وحضى معظم بلاد ما بين

(ب)

__Hamurabi__

أول تشريعة واحدة تسري على كل مملكة عرفت تلك التشريعات باسم تشريعات حمورابي وتم تقنينها ... واحدة من الأوائل من تاريخ المتكاملة من تاريخ دخل حمورابي ...

__Elamite__

وفي انتصاره عليهم من النهاية ومن فتوحاته ... وفي أواخر العصر البابلي غزو العراق (بابليين) ...

__Cushite__ (حثة)

... الدولة حاكمة لمدة حكم حوالي ___years 500___ الوسط كان هذا العصر من عصر مظلمة من تاريخ وادي الرافدين القديم العراق ...

__Mesopotamia__

الأشوريين صادق مع قيام الدولة ... قوة

جديدة في شمال العراق وهم الأشوريين ___North Iraq___ وأدت قوة عظيم الأشورية وتحولت مملكة وثور إلى أمبراطورية وقوة عظمى لقرون وكانت مدينة نينوى ___Ninvah___ عاصمة الأشوريين

___Shalmanzar___ ... ملك شمص الأول ___Assyrian___ الأشوريين من أعظم ملوك الأشورية وهو مؤسس الإمبراطورية ___Assyrian___

__Mitanni__ في بلاد الشام والحبشين ودخل في حروب كثيرة مع ... __Anatolian__ الأناضول __Hittitian__ الأشوريين هو ملك ... ___Sargon II___ ثاني أشتهر ملك

مدينة دور ... ___Dor Shroken___ وبجانب ___king Sargon___ من أعظم ملوك إنجازات ملك ...

حدود الإمبراطورية الأشورية وقام في حملات عسكرية في أرمينيا وبابل وفنيق (فينيقيا) وعلى بعض المدن نوبانيه في أنصول ومن ملوك الأشوريين ___Sennacherib___ الذي أسل أول طائر يمني

وحصار مدينة أورشليم في تلك فترة كانت مصر هي عرض الحدود لك ...

تكمله خط صفحه ٥٠٤

تكمله الأشوريين

وكان كل منهم يحاول فرض سيطرته ونفوذه في منطقة شرق الدنيا وبلاد الشام لذلك فمن ملوك الأشوريين أسرحدون Esar hadon نحو تحويل كل الكنانات أشور العسكرية في حملته لقهر مصر الذي كان يحكم في تلك فتره الملك طهارقا من king Thrka الكوشيه cushite وبالفعل نجح الملك أسرحدون king Esrhdon في اهزامه الملك طهارقا king Thrka في معركة عظيمه ونجح في غزو مصر وقضى على الأمبراطورية الأشورية وتعرف هذه الأشوريين للمصريين أصبحت أمبراطورية أشورية هي قوة أعظم وأقوى في أشرق الدنيا القديم وصلت أمبراطورية الأشورين لقمه مجدها في عهد أشور بانيبال Asshur Banibal أشور باسبال Asshur baniba اكثر ملوك الأشوريين ثقافة حتى أنه قام بتأليف أهم الكتب واسس مكتبه في مدرسه نينوى Ninvah كانت من أعظم مكتبات في العالم وذلك فته لكن بعد ملك أشوريا بسال درأت ترخل أمبراطورية أشورية في مرحله من أضطرابات من خارج أنهكت قويرها وأدت مقاطرا في نهايه من جميع الجوانب في أتحادهم مع الفرس البابلية وماداي أبراسه ومع بعض ممالكت الأحتل وأسقطو ممالكة أشورية العصر البابلي الحديث بقيادة المديش ماداي Madis والبابلي Babl سنة 613 ق.م وبدأت تظهر قوة جديده في وادي رافدين وهم البابلي هو أخر عصور ازدهر في حضاره العادي العادي الأردني ويسمى أنصا بالأمبراطوريه البابلية الحديثه الذي أسسها الملك نابوتنأسر الكلدا Nabucnazer's سنه 627 ق.م ويعتبر ملك أبجار ان نبوخذنصر من أعظم ملوك بابل كان للملك نبوخذنص ممارته كبيره مرا بوابة عشتار وحدائق المعلقه التي أعتبرها بوابتين وأحده من عجائب الدنيا السبعه وكان ملك نبوخذنص فتوحات كبيره في بلاد الشام والأناضول وهلال الخصيب أشهر نبوخذنص في تورة مرتين "بأرسال جيش على مملكه يهودا وقام بتدمير ها في حمله ثانيه ونهب عاصمه أورشليم وقام بتدمير هكل سليمان ويسمى يهود وقادهم ليكونوا عبدا في بابل تبام السبي 594 ق.م قبل ميلاد في عهد ملك نبوخذنص تجدد صراع بين بابل ومصر على شرق أدنى وأجه ملك نبوخذنص ملك مصر طهارقا ثاني في عدده معارك

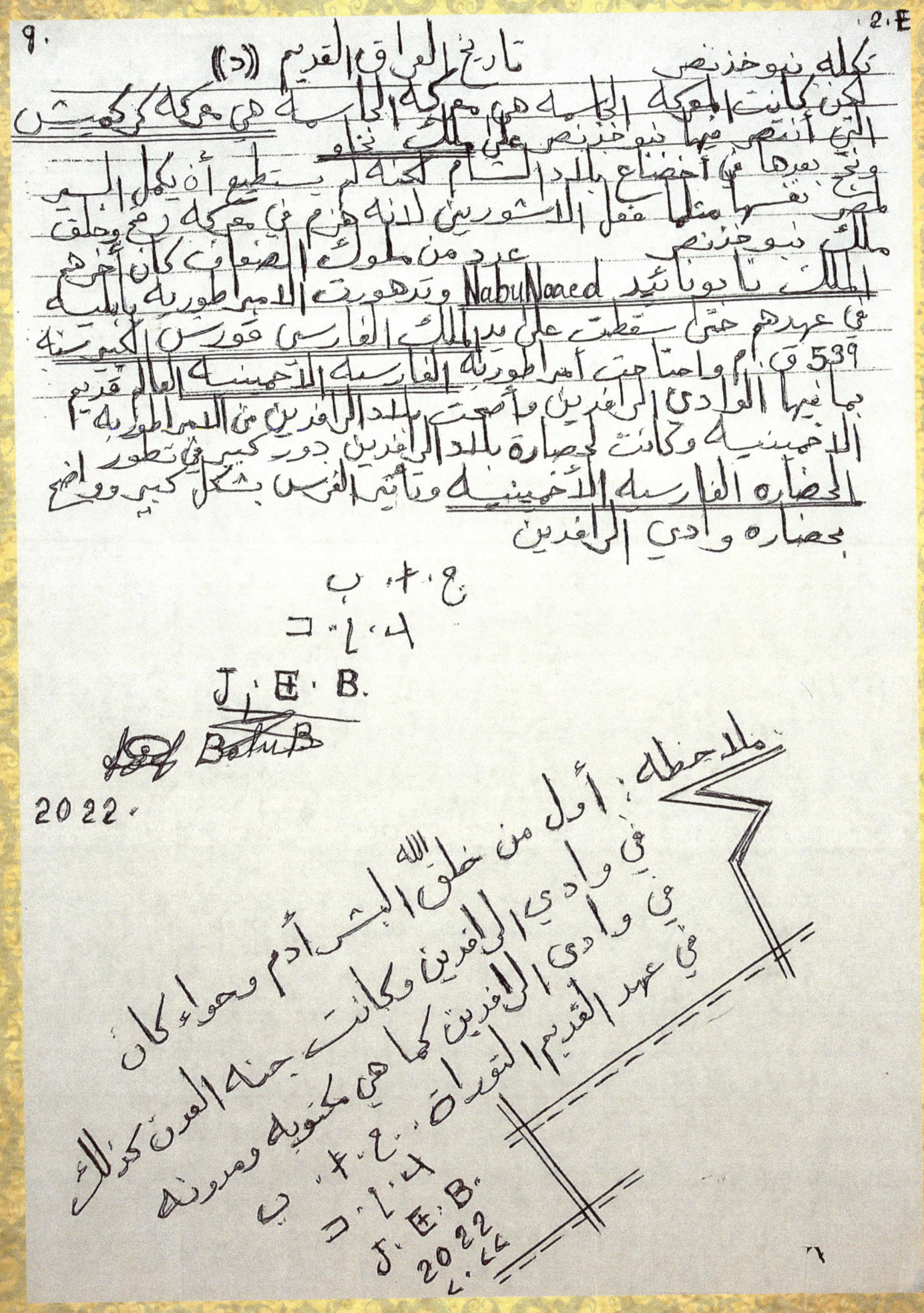

٩.

٢.E

كله نبوخذ نصر

لكن كانت معه الآلهة هي مملكة هي مملكة كوتش

الذي أنصر ... نبو خذ نصر على ... نفل

وبعدها أخضع للدولة ... الكلدانية ... أن يكون الم

نصر مثل نبو نصر ... فعل الآشوريين لدينه ... مملكته ... وخلق

ملك ... نابو نائيد كان أخ

NabuNaaed

... عهدهم حتى سقطت على يد الملك الفارسي قورش الكبير

٥٣٩ و واحتلت إمبراطورية الفارسية الأخمينية العالم القديم

بما فيها الوادي الرافدين وأصبحت بلاد الرافدين من الإمبراطورية

الأخمينية وكانت لحضارة بلاد الرافدين دور كبير في تطور

الحضارة الفارسية الأخمينية وثائبة الفرس بشكل كبير وواضح

بحضارة وادي الرافدين

ع.ت.ب
م.ل.ك
J.E.B.
Batub
2022.

ملاحظة: أول من خلق الله

في وادي الرحمن آدم وحواء كان

في وادي الرافدين وكانت منه العرب كربلاء

في وادي الرافدين كما هي مكتوبة ومدونة في عهد القديم التوراة كما هي مكتوبة ومدونة

ع.ت.ب
م.ل.ك
J.E.B.
2022.

٦

هل تعلم

الدنمارك أصغر بلد في العالم يأتي المرتبة الدولى .

* الدنمارك تقى الأرض المأهوله لعدكن الشر منذ BC-12500
* دانمارك أكبر علم في عالم ولم يتر تغيره منذ 1111 فننقول
* الدنمارك علم منفصله نظاما للحكم معا يشترا كوس بن هاكن
* وعدد سكانها جمله ونصف مليون نسه 5½ م ن
* الديانة الرسميه في الدنمارك مسيحيه و مئانيته 100% 8
و 4/100 أربعه من المانه ديانة إسلامه

عراق

* الدائنه أمتم دين في جنوب العراق في العالم الدين يأخذون ون
أدم وشنت ومالح
* أل القرن الـ 14 أو 12 كانت تعتبر بغداد المدينه أكثر
العالم ومدينه الدولى وصول تعداد ديتها ورميس بن نه
* أول تلفزيون في الشرق الاوسط هو في العراق عام 1945
في عصر ملك فصل الثاني أفتتح ملك فصل الثاني محطه
تلغزيونه من شرق الاوسط 1956 م بين المصر والسعوده
الذي أتخو التلغزيون 1965
* تم أنشأ أول دستور في العالم وتأسس أول دوله مدنه
في التاريخ أول علمه في عبد السومرين (جنوب) في
العراق * تم تأسيس أول تعلم في بابل (نظام) * تم أنشأة أولى
تأسين أول عالم تاريخ الممرس العالم * وهذا بمعول النان من عنائب
الوضع أولى في العالم * أولا نظام الصرف بابل * أول قانون
التشريع مله أحمى) * أول من أختر عو الكتابه * أول قانون دني
في نينوى * تمتلك عل أكثر أحشاط بشعول في عالم
ول يعيش في بغداد أكبر مكتبه في العالم تاريخ القديم مكتبه بيت الحكمه
** أول مكتبه ق. م في العالم مكتبه أشور بانيبال في شمال
العراق نينوى ـ ك ـ 2 . 7 . 4 . ك . 1 .

BC-12500
منذ
1111 فننقول

5½ م ن

100% 8
4/100

1945

1956 م
1965

J.E.B.

ELAMITES

عِلَام
أُمَّة

Elam: Son
of Sam
1· ch· 1:17-18

Who were the Elamites?

* J *E* B *

History

* ﺣ* ﻟ *ﺮ *

Ancient Elam

* ﻟ *†* ﻟ *

هل نقلم

ب اللہ علیہ سلام J.E.B **ELAM (Elamite)** Son of Sam x:۹

* Elam is South of IRAN Capital of Elam is Susa. ل.

* Cuneiform text read "NIM-MA-ki" in Summer. نیم ما کی

High And Land

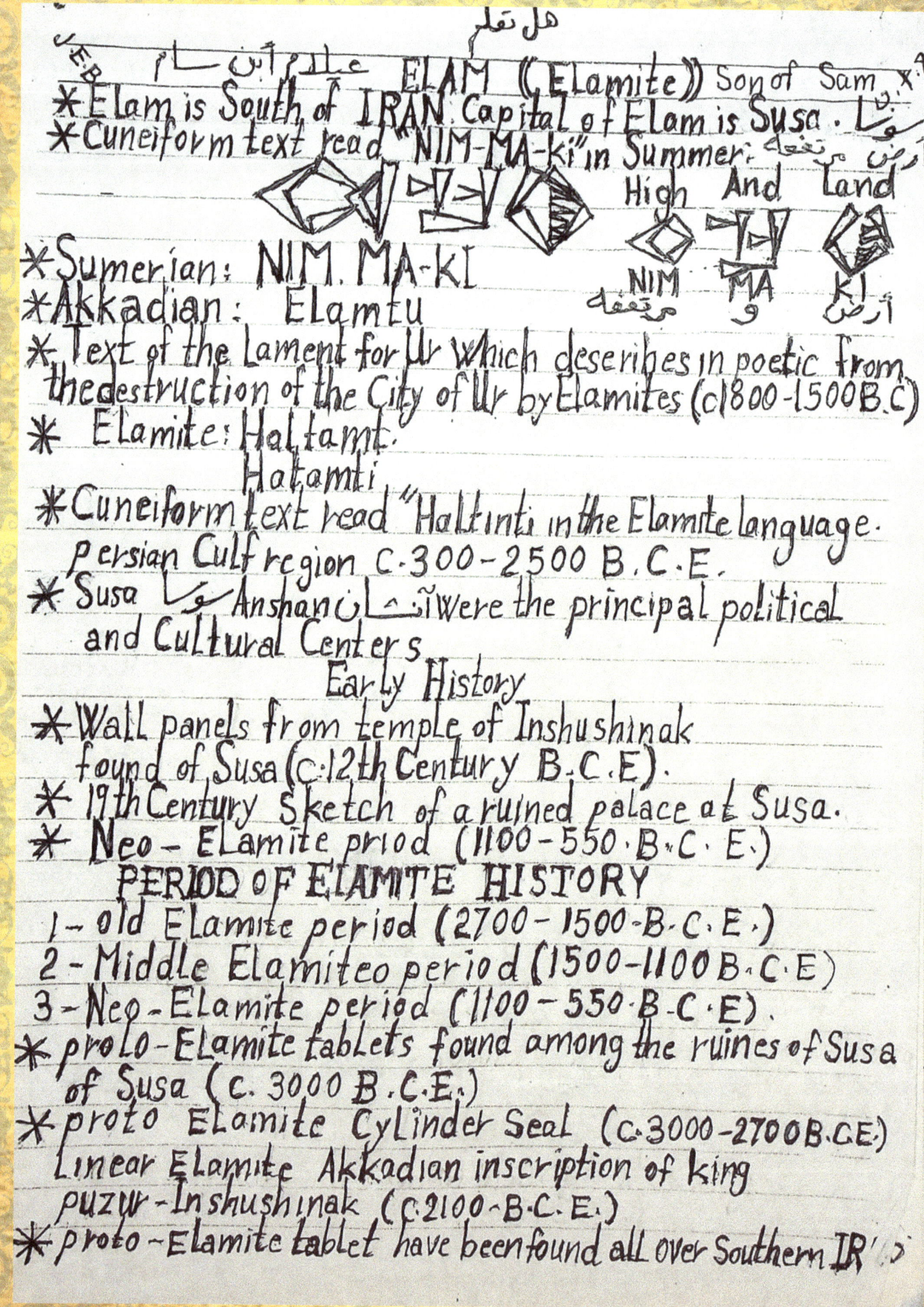

* Sumerian: NIM. MA-KI

* Akkadian: Elamtu

* Text of the Lament for Ur which describes in poetic from the destruction of the City of Ur by Elamites (c1800-1500 B.C)

* Elamite: Haltamt.
       Hatamti

* Cuneiform text read "Haltnti in the Elamite language. Persian Culf region c.300-2500 B.C.E.

* Susa لـ Anshan لـ ـ ٙ were the principal political and Cultural Centers

Early History

* Wall panels from temple of Inshushinak found of Susa (c.12th Century B.C.E).

* 19th Century Sketch of a ruined palace at Susa.

* Neo-Elamite priod (1100-550.B.C.E.)

PERIOD OF ELAMITE HISTORY

1- Old Elamite period (2700-1500.B.C.E.)

2- Middle Elamiteo period (1500-1100 B.C.E)

3- Neo-Elamite period (1100-550.B.C.E).

* proto-Elamite tablets found among the ruines of Susa of Susa (c. 3000 B.C.E.)

* proto Elamite Cylinder Seal (c.3000-2700B.CE.) Linear Elamite Akkadian inscription of king puzur-Inshushinak (c.2100-B.C.E.)

* proto-Elamite tablet have been found all over Southern IR

Elam. كلام عيلام

* proto Elamite Art (c 3200 - 2700 B.C. Bronze & Silver
* The Sumerians and Elamite for most of thier early
  history wear trading partners.
* As both side had goods and resources that the other
  coverted armed conflicts eventudly broke out between
  Sumer and Elam.
* The "Blau Monument" depicting commercial transactions
  (c 3300 - 3000 B.C.E; from Uruk, IRAQ).
* Rendition of an old Elamite seal.
  (c. 3000. B.C.E) ((British Museum London))
* Tablets from the Reign of En-Mebgragesi of kish
  mention conflicts with Elam as well as his victory
  over the Elamites (c 2700 B.C.E.).
* The Sumerian king List mentions three kings Form
  as once having outhority over Sumer and Akkad.
* Depiction of Eannatum of Lagash from the Stele
  of Vultures (c. 2450 B.C.E.)
  Eannatum claims to have chased Elamite Invaders
  out of Sumer and back of Elam
* Gu'abba was possibly the Largest Seaport in the
  persion Gulf rigion during the Middle Bronze Age.
* Gold and Silver Elamite objects (c 3100 - 1500 B.C)
* Der and Lagash, among others were popular
  destination for good going to and coming from Elam.

HITTITE KINGS ((1500 - 1450 B.C.E.))

1- Alluwamna
2- Tahur waili
3- khant, li li
4- Zidanta li
5- khuzziya li

Peace on Earth. J.E.B

القدس أرض السلام

Philistines

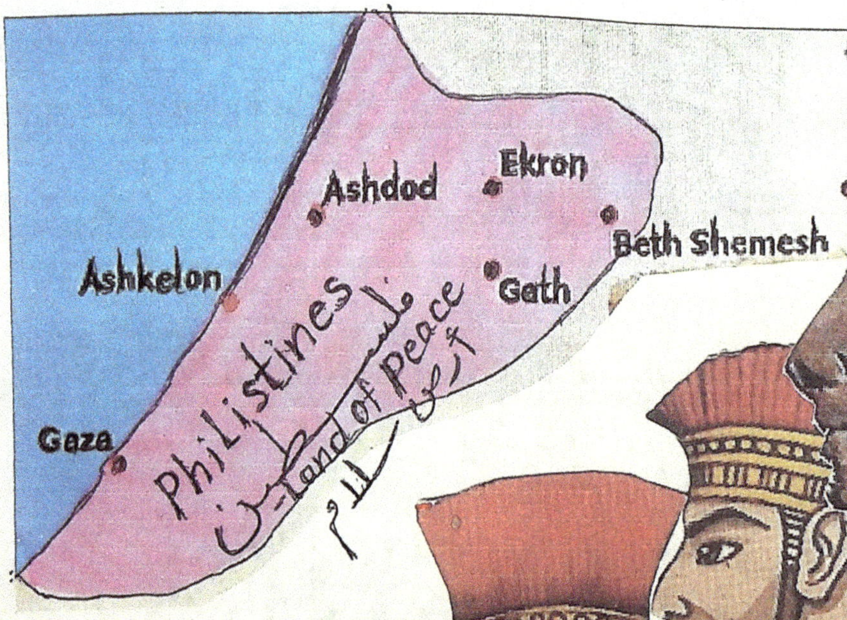

History

THE PHILISTINES

they came from

ب * أ * ج * د * أ * ل

* J * E * B *

2022

J.E.B

هذه المعلومات من كتاب مقدس عهد القديم القورات وليست من ب.ت.ع.

The Philistines فلسطين
Sea people (peleset (c. 1155 B.C.
((فلسطيا))

1-Sherden. 2-Shekelesh. 3-Ekwesh. 4-Teresh.
      5-pelste   6-Lukka.

✱ Southwestern Cannan. (c. 1150 B.C.

1-Gaza. 2-Ashkelon. 3-Ashdod. 4-Ekron 5 Gate.
The five Cities of Ashdod. Ekron. Ashkelon. Gat
and Goth former what scholars Call the
" Philistin pentapolis "
    In Book of Amos ch. 9. phers 7. Come from Chapter
Greek Island (Creet) (peleset)

    ✱ Seven Cities of plististines:
1-Gaza. 2-Ashkelon 3-Ashdod. 4-Ekron 5-Beth Shemesh
    ٥-بيت شمش ٤-إيكرون ٢ أشدود ٢- عكيلون ١- غزه
     6-Gath. 7-Hebron
     ٧- حبرون. ٦-غاث

                               ✱ الكنعان

✱ Caanan god. Dejon
✱ Neo Assyrian Rrul. (c. 704 - 612 B.C.
✱ Neo-Babylonian 604 - 539 B.C.
✱ persian (Achoemenid) rule (c. 539 - 333 B.C.
✱ Creek drachma minted in Ashdod.
   (c. 4th Century B.C. British Museum London
        ((Halonaist))

1- The few short Suriving philistine لغة
2- Inscription are in Languge Similar to Semitic Canaanite or
    كنعانية or phoenician فينيقية
3- No clear Aegean Influence on religion.
A- We dont know alot abut thire Language. B- Quickly Switched to
Speaking Canaanite out necessity. C- Many Canaanite women raised
the Next philistine generation.

History of the Hurrian Kingdom of the Mitanni

MITANNI

J.E.B

17

Mitanni king List اكراد; Zagrus من جبال مثاني

* Mitanni people from Zagaros mountain.

1- kirta
2 Suttarna 1.
3 Parrattarna 1
4 - parsatatar 1
5 - Saushtatar

* Consalidotion of Hurrian States into the Mitanni (c.1700 - 1550 B.C.E.

* Mitanni Cylinder Seal (c. 1500 - 1400 B.CE)

* Hurrian Minor kingdoms principlites and States (c. 1900 - 1650 B.C.).

* Akkadian Empire of Naram-Sin (c 2250~ B.C.

* Neo - Sumer Empire of Shulgi (c. 2000 B.C.

* Empire of Shamshi - Adad (c. 1775. B.C.

* Consalidation of Hurrian States into the Mitanni Cc. 1700 - 1550 B.C.

* Mitanni Cylinder Seal (c. 1500 - 1400. B.C.

* order clashes between Mitanni - Hurrian and Hittite forces increas (c. 1550 - 1500 B.C.

Neo Elamite period - Elomite Vs Assyrian (1100-550 B.C.

Neo-Elamite kings:-   Neo-Assyrian king

Neo-Elamite kings	Neo-Assyrian king
1-Humban-nikash (743-717 B.C.	1-Tiglath-pileser III. 745-727.B.C
2-Shutruk Nahhunte II (716-699 B.C.	2 Shalmaneser V. 726-722 B.C.
3-Hallushu (699-693.B.C.	3-Sorgon II. 721-705 B.C.
4-Kutir-Nahhunte II (693- B.C	4-Sennacherib. 704-681-B.C
5-Huban-Nimena III (692-689 B.C	5- Esarhaddon. 680-669.B.C.
6-Huban-Haltash I. (688-681 B.C.	6 Ashurbanipal 668-630 B.C.
7-Huban-Haltash II (680-675.B.C.	7-Ashur-Etil-ilani 630-625.B.C.
8-Urtak (674-664 B.C.	8-Sin-Sum-Lishir 626-625 B.C.
9-Te-Ummon (664-653.B.C	9-Sin Sarra-Ishkun 624-612 B.C.
10-Huban-nikash II (652-649 B.C.	10-Ashur-Uballit II. 612-610 B.C.
11-Ind-bigash (649-648 B.C.	
12-Humban-Haltash III (648-642 B.C.	

GUDEA OF LAGASH

Gudea of Lagash. Ancent Sumer Enlightend king

*Gudea of Lagash

I remitted debts & Washed all Hands of Such Obligations For Seven days no Grain was ground the Slave Gril Was equal to her Mistress & the Slave Stood at his master's Side The Orphan Was not given over to the Wealthy mane; the Widow Was Not given over to the powerful man; & in the hous With no male heir its daughter became its heir - Gudea of Lagash. r. 2144-2124 B.C.

He (Gudea) struck the Cities of Anshon اﻧﺸﺎن and Elam ﻋﻴﻼم With Weapon and brought their Spoil into the Eninnu of Ningirsu. on the day When GUDEA the ruler of LAGASH had Finshed bulding the Eninnu for Ningirus, he mad the Spoil s a permonat dontion to the temple - Inscription of GUDEA.

5:15pm. Sat. Oct. 1. 2022. J. E. Bohri Bek. J-E-B. ٠٩٢٠٠JJH

MARI

Mari started حصاره مار

The History of the Magnificent city of مار مدينة قديمة من السومر في جنوب

Ancient Sumer /Akkad /Babilonia. وادي الرافدين

Anbu king of MARI

in Mari Anbu became king and ruled For 30 years Anba ANEA the Son of ANBU reigned For 17 years BAZI the Leather Worker reiged For 30 years ZIZI the fuller reigned For 20 years Limer the anoited prist, reigned For 30 year Sharrum-iter reignd For 9 years Then MARI Was defeated and the kingship taken to KISH Sumerian king Listed.

* Cylinder Seals & Seal Impressions c. 2700-2600
* Artist Conception of MARI   Louver Museum. paris
      (c. 2900-2500 B.C.E
* Statue of EBIH·II·Superintendent of MARI
          (c. 2500-2334. B.C. Louver Museum. paris
* Statue of Ishqi-Mari. the Last king of Mari. befor Sargon of Akkad · (c. 2340-2330 Aleppo Museum.
* Head of Sargon (or possibly his grandson, Naram-Sin)
   (c. 2300-2200 B.C. IRAQ nationl Museum, Baghdad)
* MARI (c. 2300-2250·B.C.
* Statue of the Shakkanakku ruler Iddi-Ilum
* (c. 2100-200·B.C. Louver Museum. paris)
* Statue of puzur. Ishtar, the Shakkangkku, ruler of Mari.(c 2050 B.C. Museum of Ancient Orent, Istanbul

MARI

Mari From page.9. ‏(٩)‏ ‏كتابة مار من صفحة‏
Amorite king of Mari ‏ملوك أموريين من مار سنة‏
‏من سومر، وادي رافدين‏

AMORITE KING of MARI

1 - Yahdun - Lim   C. 1810 - 1794 · B.C.
2 - Sumu - Yamam   C. 1793 - 1792 - B.C
3 - Yasmah - Addu   C. 1782 - 1775 B.C.
   Son and Viceroy of Shashi - Adod.
4 - Zimri - Lim   C. 1774 - 1762 B.C.

Letter from Shamshi - Adad.

I gave you this City. Why do you ask to decid this matter?
If you are able to Hold this City, hold it. If you are Not
there are many others Who have enugh energy to hold it
I will not obandon my hous to administer yous. A reol man
must adminster his own house

‏رسالة من‏ Letter from Shamshi Adad to his Son ‏الى ابنه‏
‏شَمِش أداد‏ Yosmah - Addu (a.k.a Yasman Adad.) ‏ياسَم أداد‏

* Sculpture of lion from the palace of Zimri - Lim
  (c. 1775 - 1763 B.C. Louver museum. paris.
* Foundation peg of Rim - Sin
  (c. 1822 - 1763) Trustees of the Britsh Museum London
* Head of an Amorite ruler belived to be Hammurabi
  (c. 1750 B.C. Louver Museum. paris)
* Ruins of Mari's Ziggurat
* Tablet from Mari's archives
  (c. 1780 - 1763; Louve Museum paris)

‏ن·ī·ح·‏ J.E.B. ‏ا·خ·ﻻ‏
oct. 2 - 2022.

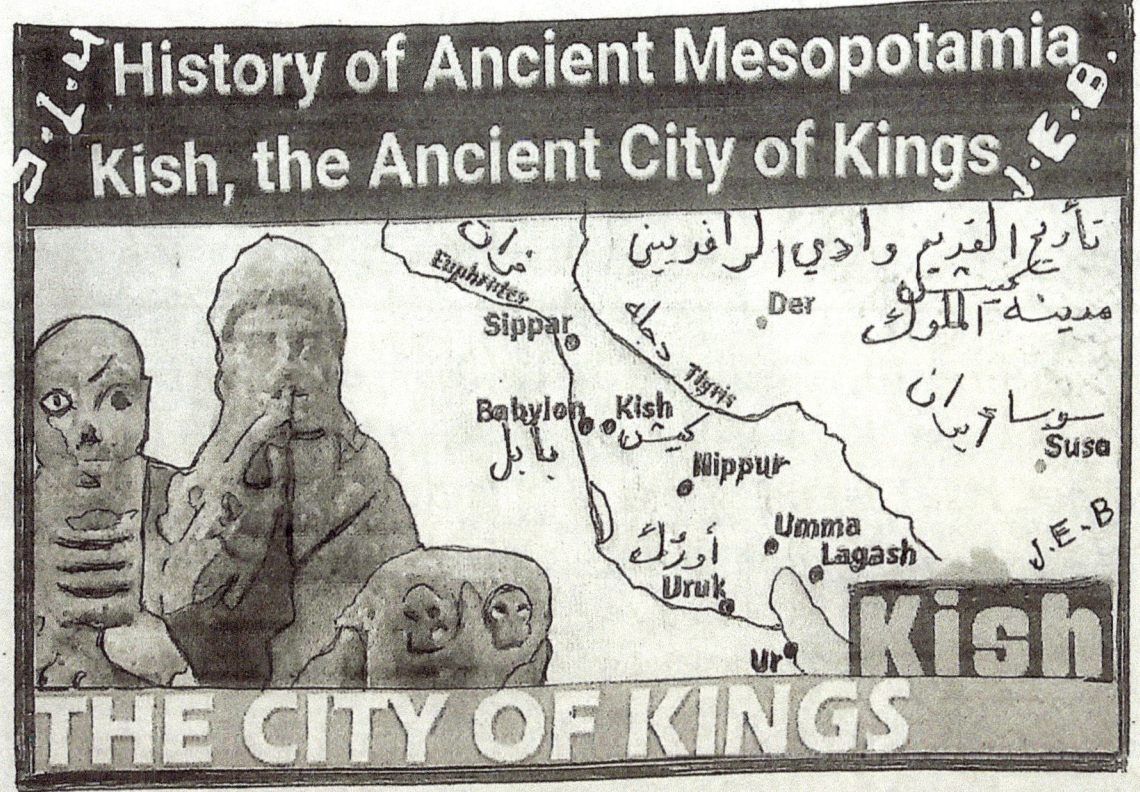

KISH
kish.

kish: the Ancient City of king. History of Ancient of Mesopotamia / Sumer / Akkad

* Figurine of Man (c. 200-1600 B.C. Louver Museum paris
* Ruine of kish's great Zigguart.
* Ubid artifact from kish. (c. 5300-3700. B.C. Louver. paris

Sumerian kigs List

After the flood had Swept Over the Land and the kingship had once agane descended from the heavens, the Seat of kingship Was in the City of kish. in kish, Gishur becme king and reigned for 1,200 years. kullasina-bel reigned for 900 years.

Sumerian king List.

* Seal of Mesannepanda of Ur With title king of kish (c. 2500 B.C. penn Museum, philadelphia. U.S.A.)
* Partial text reading "Mes-an-hipadda, Lugal Kiski, dam-nu-gig-oi." Mesannepada, king of kish, his Wife."
* Anciet Sumer (c. 3000-2300) B.C.
* kish Civiluzation (. c. 300-2500). B.C.
* AKKADIAN Empire (c. 2300 B.C.)
* "Sargon, king of kish was Victorious in thirty-four battles. He destroyed City Walls all the Way to the Shore of the Sea

Inscription of Sargon.

* Akkadian-Language text from kish
c. 2300-2200 B.C. Louver Museum. paris,
" in kish, they raised Up Iphur-kishe to kingship and in Uruk, they raised Up Amar-girid to kingship as Well" filled the Euphrates River with them and conquered the City of kish and destroyed its Walls. Further, he made the rever run over inside it and slew 2,525 men in City." Inscription of Naram-Sin.
* Neo-Sumerian Cylinder Seal & Sea Impression c. 2100-2000 B.C. Louver paris

UR

Ur a Short   Ur. أور

History of Great Sumerian City

The ruine of Ur's great Ziggurat, the Sumerian world's Greatest temple dedicated to the <u>moon god Nannalii</u> الاله

* Ur Abrahams
* Ur May Be Over 7000 Years Old
* Objects found during excavations at the Site of Tel Muqayyar a.k.a. Ur.
* Excavation of Tel al-Uhymir, IRAQ (Ancient Kish)
* Excavations of Tel el-Muquayyer (Ur)

        Ubaid period
        C. 5500-4000 B.C.
        Early Dynastic priod
        C. 2900-2334. B.C.

* Deseent into the depthe of the Royal Cemetery of Ur. (Woolly & his tea 1922-1934))
* The famous "Standard of Ur. (c.2600-B.C.E. British Museum London)
* Objects found in "Royal Cemetery" of Ur   c.2600 B.C.E. British museum London
* Early type of board game found in the Royal Cemetery"
       (c. 2600-B.C.E. British Museum -London)
* Territories and tributaries of <u>Sargon</u> the Great   c.2300. B.C
* Depiction king of <u>Ur-Nammu</u> withe god Enlil
    (c. 2112-2004. B.C. penn Museum, philadelphia. U.S.A.)
* Votwe tablet and cylinder seal of king Shulgi of Ur
    (c.2004. B.C.E. British Museum, London).
* Temple foundation pegs of Ur-Nammu and Shulge
    (c. 2112-2004. B.C.E. Metropolitan Museum of Art. New York. U.S
* <u>Territores & tributaries of the Neo-Sumerian Empire of Shulgi</u>
    (c. 2094-2047 B.C.E.)

أور . Ur . From page 23 تكملة من صفحة

Third Dynasty of Ur

1- Ur-Nammu	2112 - 2095 . B.C
2 - Shulgi	2094 - 2047 . B.C.
3 - Amar - Sin	2046 - 2038 . B.C
4 - Shu - Sin	2037 - 2029 . B.C
5 - Ibbi - Sin	2028 - 2004 . B.C.

There wear many reason for the FALL of the
Neo-Sumerian Empire two of them being Amorite
Migration and Elamite aggresson

History of the Hurrian Kingdom of the Mitanni

MITANNI

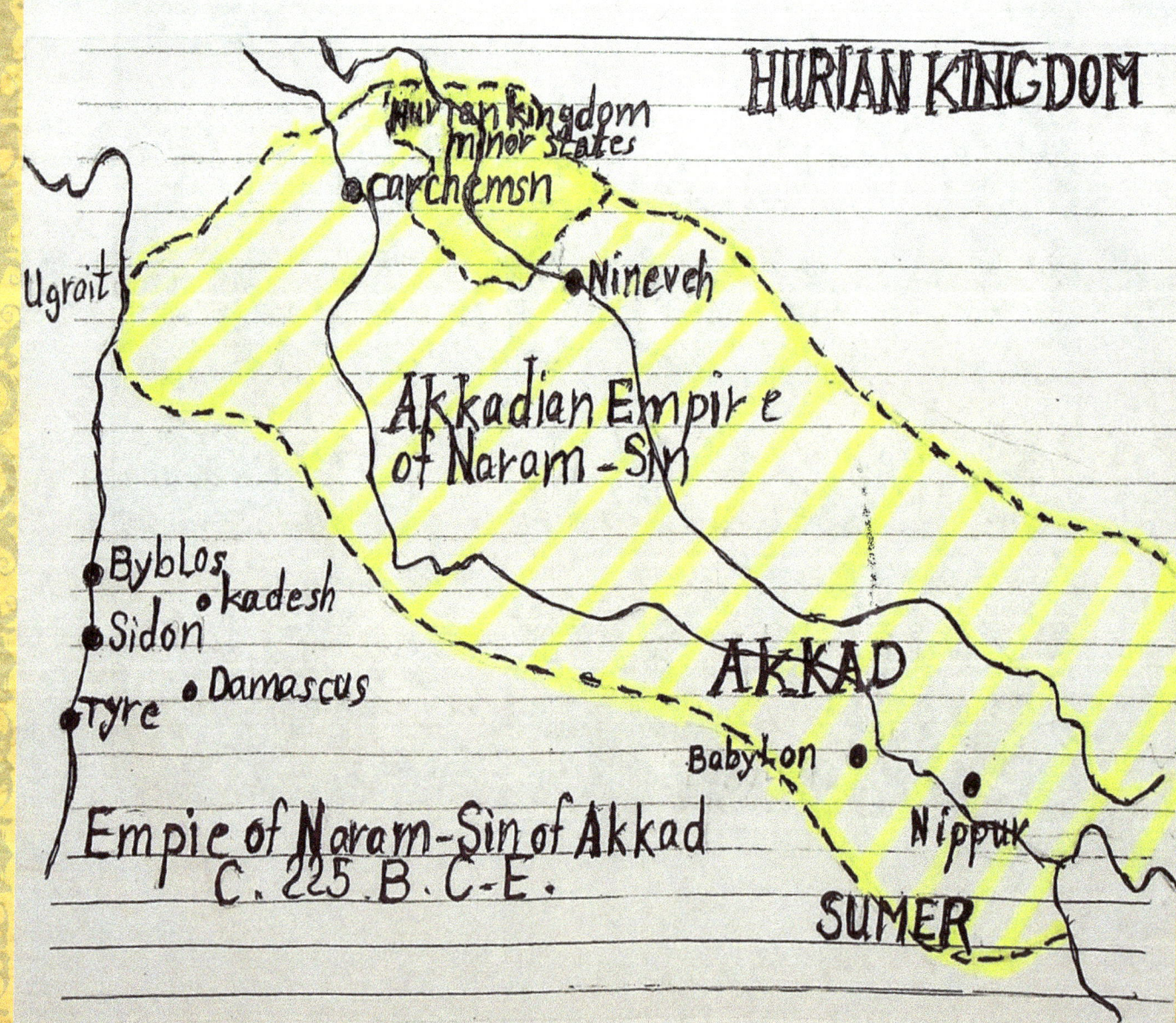

HURIAN KINGDOM

Hurian kingdom
minor states

Carchemsh

Nineveh

Ugrait

Akkadian Empire
of Naram - Sin

Byblos
kadesh
Sidon
Damascus
Tyre

AKKAD

Babylon

Nippur

Empie of Naram-Sin of Akkad
C. 225 B.C-E.

SUMER

Hurrian الحوريين

Hurrian : حوريين   Hurrian From p. 14 صفحه من   Hurrian الكا

Bulding/temple Copper foundation from Hurrian City of
Urkes c. 2200-2100 B.C.E.

⊬ ⊬ ⊬ ⊬

بلاد اناتوليا وسوريا   Hurrian هوريين عرف كيم من   هوريين عرف كيم من
تركيا (شرقها) شرق آناتوليا

Beleved to have been Composed by king Tushatta of the Mitanni
the inscription is part of what is Caled "Mitann Letter" and was
found at the Egyptian Site of EL Amarna, It accompanied the
Hurrian princess Taduepa as she went to Egypt to be
Marred to pharaoh Amenhotep III c. 14th Century B.C.E.
* The translation reads:
"As my brother now Loves me and as I now Love my brother,
   my they, the gods Tešub, Sayška, Amanu, Simige and
Ea-Šarri, love us Very much in their hearts"
* Urartian inscription of Argisti c. 787-766 B.C.
* Map of Kingdom of Urartu 780 B.C. خارطة مملكة اورارتو *
* Relief of Hurrian Camel rider c. 1000 B.C.
* Empire of Naram-Sin of Akkad c. 2250 B.C.
* Dedication tablet to the god Nergal Commisoined by the
Hurrion king Atalshen of Urkesh c. 2000 B.C.E.
* Ruins of the Anciant Hurrian City of Urkes Tel Nozan Syria.
1- Sketch of Seal of Harrian king of Urkes, Tupkish. Sep 2022
2- Sketch of Seal of From Urkesh.
   Hurrian word for king آنزان endan معنى كلمة آنزان ملك الله
* Fragment of Stele depicting Naram-Sin of Akkad c. 2250 B.C.
* Victory Stele of Narman Sin. c. 2250 B.C.
* Collapse of the Akkadian Empire bring Indepenence to Hurrian state in
   Northern Moesopotamia.
* Neo-Sumerian Empir and tributaries of King   * Empire of Shamsh-Adad-r. 1796-1775 B.C.
Shulgi of Ur c. 2000 B.C.   of Eastran Anatolia & Northern Syria.
* Many Hurrian migrated twest to part of Eastran Anatolia & Northern Syria.
* Hurrian are Unity to form the kingdom Mitanni c. 1500-14008.C.

اُردو

ERIDU

The City of Erido and Significance in Sumer Myth and history Ancient Mesopotmia

"After the kingship descended from Heven the kingship Was Eridu, Aluim became king; he ruld for 28,800 years. Ala Lar ruld for 36,000 years. Two king, they ruled, for a total of 64,800 years Then Erid fell and the kingship Was taken to Bad-tibira. Sumerian king List هذه الواثقة كتاب

* Sumerian king List from Larsa من قائمة ملك (Weld-Blundell prism) (c.1800, B.C. Ashmole Museum Oxford)
* Eridu Inhabinant it had been As far back 8000 B.C. 10,000 years ago. * Enki god frash Water and kowlege
* pottery shards from Eridu. c.5000-3500 B.C. Lover museum paris
* Cylinder Seal Impression with depiction of the god Enki c.2250 B.C. Trustees of British Museum London.
* Ancent Sumer c.3000-2500 B.C.
* Irick from Eridu Comissioned by king Amar-Sin of the Ur III dynst 2046-2038 B.C. Louver museum, paris
* Neo-Sumerian Empire of the third Dyasty of Ur Under king Shulgi c.2050 B.C.
* The Adda Seal with a dcpicton of god Enki c.2300 B.C. Britsh Museum London.

oct-2022 ن.ف.غ J.E.B. ﮊ.ﻝ.ﺡ

NUBIA نوبيا

Ancient NUBIT   kingdom of KUSH
Egyptian depiction of Nubian with a graffe on Monkey
(c. 1500 - 1425 B.C)
The desert of Nubia Jast outside of MEROË

NUBIA
What is Name Nubia
Come
The word "nub" means
gold in the Ancient
Egyptian Languge

أوكلمة نوب مصرى من اللغة
أوكلمة مصرية قديمة
ذهب

Egypt مصر
Red Sea
Saud Arbia السعودية
عمان
اليمن
NUBIA نوبيا
Sudan سودان
Gulf of Aden
Arabian Sea

The term could also come from the names of the tribes that
Settled in the region, The NUBA or the Nobo نوبة
Nubia   أُنها أيضاً قد تكون أسمَ قبائل
NUBIAN : النوبى
procession of Nubians depicted on the Wall of a tomb
(c. 1220 B.C. Luxor. Egypt) نوبيا وكوش ع قبة ع بعض
معلومات عن نوبيا حاثة من مصر الم

* Woll from the Incide of TOMB of Queen Oalhala
   C. 700 - 650. B.C, Royal Cemetery of el-kurru. Sudan)
* The desert of Nubia Just out Side of MERE
* Reconstruction of Nabia ploya (ATENDAR Circle
   C c. 7500 B.C.E Aswan Nubian Museum Aswan
Outline of Scen Carved in Stone from Gebel Sheikh
Sulmeman جبل شيخ سلمان c. 3500 - 300 B.C. khartoum Museum)
* Incent burner found in Upper Nubia South first cataract
   (c. 3800 - 3100 B.C. University of Chicago, chicago)
d. Oct. 5 - 2022   · J.E.B.   ب.٢.٤.ج.ٕ.٤

From page 29 في صفحة Nubia. النوبة

* Stele depicting Amenirdi. Sister of Kashta and gods wife
c. 670 B.C.E. University of chicago. Chicgo
* 1 PLANKi (piye) r. 753-722. B.C
Fouder of Egyl's 25th Dynast and the First kushite king to
Simultaneously control both kush and Egypt.
2- Shabaka r. 722-707 B.C.E.)
* Due to the Assyrian threat the kushite pharaohs fored alliances
With the kingdom of Judah and Various phoenican city-Sates
* Shabataka Sent fighting men along with younger brother Taharqa
to aid Hezekiah of Judah and his Phoenican allies.
* Sennacherib. c.691 B.C. British Museum London
* Taharqa he Become phraoh of Egypt.
* Victory stete of Esarhadon   انتصار أسرهدون
(c. 671 B.C. pergamon Museum, Berlen)
* Statuett of Taharqa and the falcon god, Horus c. 670 B Lover. paris
* KINGS featured include Tantamani, Taharqa, Senkamanisken,
Tanamani, Aspelta, Anlamani and Senkamanisken.
* Statue of Pharaoh psamtik.11. c. 590 B.C. Lover Museum paris
* Aruond 590 B.C. Egyption Captured Napata, forcin the royal
family of CUSH to flee to the City of Meröe مروي
* Meroitic Script on tablet found in Meröes, مَ
* Bronze head found in Meröe of Roman emperer
Augustus - c.27-25 B.C. British. Museum London.
* Gold Coin of king Ezan of Axum c. 340
* Runs of kushite pramids along the Nubian horizon
* kushite ruins at the Site of Muswwarat al-Sufra وف
* Statue of a kushite pharaoh 700 B.C Metropolitan Museum of Art NewYork
* Head of a king kushite. رأس ملك كوشي

12:36 Am. Thu. oct 6 - 2022   تقريبا ٢٧ دقيقة منتصف الليل
Oct. 6. 2022   J.E.B.

تكملة Nubia صفحة ٣٠ from pege 30 تكملة نوبيا . نوبيين . نوبي

Between 2500-2400 B.C the Egyptian established Several
Colonies مستعمرات in Nubia نوبيا purpose of Smelting copper & Gold
* Around 2100 B.C armed Conflicts between the Egyptian and
Nubian Tribes قبائل نوبين Increased. صراع مابين مصريين ونوبيين
* Ruins of the City of kerma Just South of the Third Cataract in
Modern Sudan (2400 B.C)
* Copy of Tomb depicting Captiy Nubian on Ship.
(c.1350 B.C Metropolitan Museum of Art, New York City
* Ruin in kerma of large religious Structur known as the Westen Deffufa
Nubian archer found in governor's tomb in Asyut (c. 2000 B.C Egyption Museum Cairo)
* Depiction of the Hyksos from Tomb of khnumbtcall c. 1900 B C.E.)
* kamose r 1555-1550 B.C Brother of Ahmos (pharoh)
* Head of pharaoh Ahmos C 1555-1525 B.C Museum of New York City
* Territores of Egypt and Nubia Controlled By phraoh فرعون
Ahmose C. 1525 B.C.
* Wall mural depcting pharoah فراعنة Ramises II رمسيس in bottle
against Nubian نزاع ملك فرعون رمسيس ضد نوبيين
c. 1330 B.C Temple of Beit-el Wali, Nubion.) مصر أحتلو*
* Egyption occupied Nubia and kush (أحتلت) نوبيين وكوش
* pyramids Amongst the Ruins of Napatas Royal Cemetery of
Nuri
* Ruin columns at Site of Jebal جبل Burkal,
* The political instabil instability of Egypts Third intemediate
period c. 1069-525 B.C allwed kushites to gain
greater Automony
* First king of kush to be mentoined
by name any Written documents or inscription
1- AIARA r. 785-765 B.C. First king of KUSH.
2- KASHTA (Brother of Alora) r. 765-753 B.C. Conquered
part of Upper Egypt Up the City of Theba
3- pianki r. 753-722 B.C. Founder of Egypt's 25th Dynasty and
first kushite king Simultaneously control both kush & Egypt

Coptic

Coptic: The Final Ancient Egyptian langueqe

لفة قبطيه 25/100 من لفة قبطيه هى Creek يونان: تتكون
من القبط و يونان القديمه

1- Papyrus Oxyhrnchus 1

1- Papyrus Oxyhrnchus 1.   2- Nog Hommad Codex 2.
   Creek

20/100 From Egypt they Are Coptic

Ries of URUK

The Birth of Civilsation   6500 B.C.

The Birth of Civilsation

- Urbon Enviroments
- Agriculture.
- Monumental Building.
- Social Hierarchy
  Writing / Literocy

"SAG"   Head
3200-3000·B·C.   or   Appox 2800·B·C.

Inscription From 2600 B.C.   Tablet From 2600·B·C·

Lote 3rd Millennium·B·C   Early 2nd millennium B·C   Eirly 1st millenniun
                                                              B·C

The Birth of Civilisation - Rise of Uruk 6500 BC to 3200 BC

Rise of Uruk

ولاده الحضارات في وادي
الرافدين وفي أورك

J.E.B.

Cuinforn & Symboles

رموز وكتابه المسمارية

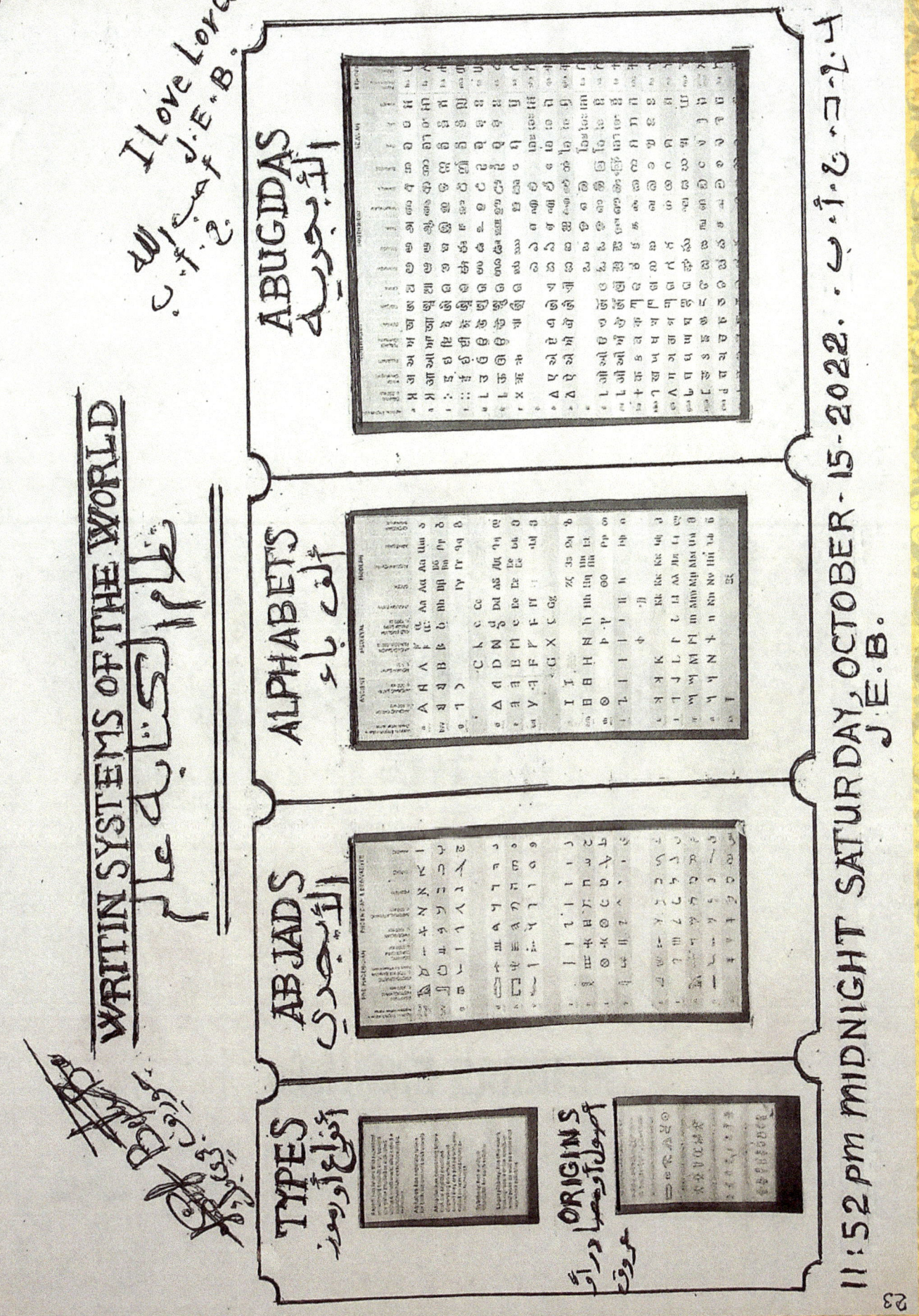

I Love Lord
J.E.B.

WRITIN SYSTEMS OF THE WORLD

ABUGIDAS الابجدية

ALPHABETS الف با

ABJADS الابجدية

TYPES

ORIGINS

إيران

IRAN

MADAI
ماداي

Madai Son
of Japheth
1ch. 1: 5-6

THE
SASSANIAN
الساسانيه

PERSIAN EMPIRE
✳ الأمبراطوريه الفارسيه ✳

The Early Medes & # The MEDES مادای
the Median Empire-

Medes From Zagros Mountains مادای زنجبره از اراده
* Depiction of two Medes from Apadana at Perspolis (parsa)
(cl. 5th Century B.C.E British Musem London)

who were the Medes?

Mad   - Old persian /Iranian languege
Medes   - Greek
Mad Madaya - Assyrian call them. Land of Mada
Medes: western IRAN.

Moving on from the land parsua, I went down to the land
of Mesu, Media (Land of the Medes) Araziash, and Havha,
and Capturd the Cities of kyakinda, Hazzanabi, Esamul
and kinabila. I massacred them thes Cities
                Annals of Shalmaneser. III.

* Statue of Shalmaneser. III
   (c. 858-824. B.C. IRAQ-Museum, Baghdad)
* Stele of Shamshi-Adad V
   (c. 822-811 B.C.E. British Museum, London)
✓ I reached the land of the Medes took fright in the face of the
angry weaponed of Ashur & my strong warfare which have n.
riva and abandoned their Cities. They ascended a rugged
mountain and pursued them. I massacred 2300 Soldiers o
Hanasiruk the Mede I took away from him 140 of Cayaly and
Carred awy his proprty and possessions in countless
quantities. Inscription of shamshi-Adad. V
* depicting Tiglath-pileser III receiving dignitaries
   (c. 5-727. Detroit-Institute of Arts. Detroit) U.S.A.

ىدام Medes From page 36. Medes دلم

I orderd my armies to march against the MEDES. As for those
City ruler, who Were not submisse, I Conqured their Cities defeated
them and took their Spoil ... As for those who did Submit, I received
their tribute. 130 horses from Bit Ishtar and its districts I received
120 horses from Cities of Giniznamu. Sadbat, Sisad ... 100 horses
from Uposh of Bit kapsi, 100 horses from Ushru of Nikist.

inscription of Tiglath-pileser III.

Neo-ASSYRIAN KINGS

Shalmaneser. V	726-722. B.C.
Sargon II	721-705. B.C.
Sennacherib	704-681. B.C.
Esarhadon	680-669. B.C.
Ashur bonipal	668-630. B.C.

To parsuash I descended. The City ruler of Namri. Son, but
Bit-Abdadant and the land of the mighty Medes, heard the
Coming of my expediton in their minds and terror fell Upon
them. Thir heavy parsuash my possession. horses fast ones fiary
myles, Bactriam famelys, offespring of their lands, large
and Smal Cattle received .. Annals of Sargon. II.
← Depiction of Sargon. II possibly Crown prince Sennacherib
(c. 710 B.C British museum. London.

On my return (from ELLipi) I recived the haevy tribut of
the distant MEDES. Whose name no one among the kings,
my fathers, had heard; to the yoke of my rule I made
then Submit." inscription of Sennachrib

"Tribut & Contributions for my lordship I imposed on them patu sharri, a
Landbordering the Salt Desert, in the midst of the land of the distant Mede
by Bikni, the lapis lazuli mountain on whose Soil none of the
kings my fathers had ever set fool
inscription of Esarhadad.

مادیا   Frompege: 37 نه دید Medes قاله

✳ Deioce , C·727-657·B·C·
  (Dahyuk Old Iranian)
                - Media ·
                - Deioces
                - phrortes

✳ Cyaxares
   (c·625-585· B·C·)
  Huvakhshtra (Old Iranian)
✳ Relief of Ashurbanipal from the <u>Great Assyrian capital of Nineve</u>
   (c·668-627· B·C·E· Museum· of London·)
✳ Cylinder of Nabolassar (c·626-605·B·C· British Museum London)
✓ In the month· of Ab (July-August), the Medes· Went along the Tigris
  & encamped against Ashur· They did batte aginst the City and inflicted
  a terrible defeat Upon a great people, plunderd and Sacked them·
  The king of <u>Akkad and his Army·</u> who had gone to help the <u>Medes,</u>
  did not reach the batte · Babylonian Chronicle·
✓ They Comped against Nineveh ·From the month of Sivan (June) Until
   the monhs the month of Ab (آب) (August, for three month they
  Subjected the City to Heavy defeat Upon a mighty people·· They Carried
  away heavy Spoils from the City and the temple· They turned the City into
  ruin heap · Babylonian Chronicle·
✳ Astyages (r·584-550 B·C· · Rshtivaga (Old Iranian)

MEDES	PERSIA
Deioces	
Phraortes	Achaemenes
Craxares	Teispes
Astyages	Cyrus
Mandane	Combyses·1·

Cyrus ·II·

* إيران : أنها الأرض الإيرانيين
** إيران : يعود تاريخها إلى 7000 الاف قبل ميلاد م
** إيران : 1936 كانت تعرف في بلاد الفارسي إلى أمست
كل علام والفارسي ومملكة الحرملة وحمل أذربيجان
وأبرز قادتها الخورش ووصل بها ابعد رقعه
* عاصمه 4 إيران طهران ومعناها تحت: تحت: وان
الأرض منطقة يصبح المعني تحت الأرض

1- أذربيجان
2- أكراد
3- كرد
4- بلوش
5- عرب
6- تركمان   7- قبائل تركية أخرى

علم إيران 1980
يتألف العلم الإيراني من ثلاثه الوان وهي :- الأخضر وأبيض والأحمر
1- لون الأخضر : الإسلام
2- لون الأبيض : الصدق والسلام
3- لون الأحمر : الشيعه والاستشهاد
4- يتركز في الأبيض (متصع) اسم الله
5- على طول حافات لون الأبيض مكتوبه
لا إله إلا الله

لون الأخضر
الإسلام

لون أبيض
صدق والسلام
الله

لون الأحمر
شيعه والاستشهاد

لا إله إلا الله
الله اكبر الله اكبر

هل تعلم :
* بمن الرز : معناها عشيه رجال Ten Man : معاها في الأنكليزي
* استكان : East : شرق . Tea : شاي . can : قوطيه
East Tea can = أو علبه ثاني شرقي + كان + شرقي East + Tea + can علبه

Ten man
10 man
كونيه
10 man

استكان

Evolution of Alph Pit — تطور الكتابة

الفينيقية Phoenician

Aramic — الآرامية

Hebrw — العبرية

Arabic — العربية

Ancient Greek — اليونانية القديمة

ABCD

Cyrillic — ΑБГД

ΑBΓΔ

oct·7-2022·
ت. أ. ع. ب.
J.E.B.

Langueges in the world

1. Tamil : التاميلية
2. Sanskript. Jainism - Buddism Indiansim.
3. Egypt: 2600 B.C.
4. Greek   1.450 B.C
5. Chinese
6. Aramaic
7. Hebrew
8. korean
9. Armenian IndEurp
10. Latin (Italic)

أرقام

Nembers

1 — I	11 — XI
2 — II	12 — XII
3 — III	
4 — IIII	
5 — V	
6 — VI	
7 — VII	
8 — VIII	
9 — IX	
10 — X	

SUN·Oct·
9-2022
J.E.P

God·EL· الله

phoanician
Hebreo

<u>History of phoenician city of</u>
<u>Sidon from Bronze age to</u>
<u>Roman pried.</u>   SIDON الصيدون

Sidon (. c 220 · B · C .
* Vas from Sidon . (c . 330 - 2100 B.C Louvre Museum paris)
* Pi ther from Sidon (C . 2100 - 1550 . B . C . Louver . paris)
Sidon . (c 2200 B . C .
Neo - Sumerian Seal Impression from Sidon .
(c 2100 - 2004 B . C . Louve Museum paris)
* One of Amarna . (العمارنا) many Letters 1400 - 1300 B.c. Louve paris
* Block with an Egyptian - Style Relif from a buiding in Sidon
(c 1000 - 7000 B.c . Louver Museum , paris).
✓ <u>Zimredda</u> the ryler of City of Sidon, has Written daily to
the rebul <u>Aziru</u> Son of Abdi-Ashiru Concernin evry word
that he has heard from the Land of Egypt.
                              Amrana Letter #147
"The one Who has raided the Land of the king is the king of
Sidon"   Amrana Letter #148
1175Bc أنتم بويين عصر سنم ص أميرالطورية حزنه بقيه   Sidon
* Tiglath - pil eser . 1 .   Assyria الله
c . 1100' B . C .
* Relief of Ashur nasirpal . II . c . 850 . B . C . British . London
* Cylinder Seal Impression from Sidon c . 1000 - 7000 . B . C . Louver paris
* Relief from the palace of Sennacherib at Nineveh . C . 704 - 681 . B . C . New York city U . S . A
✓ "<u>Luli, king of Sidon,</u> Whom the terror - inspiring glamor of my
Lordship had over Whelmed, fled for Over Seas & perished. The awe
- inspiring Splendor of the Weapon" of Ashur, my lord, over whelmed
his Strong Cities, Such as Great Sidon & Little Sidon . Installed
Ethba'al Upon the thron to be their king & imposed Upon him
: tribut due to me as his overlord to be paid annualy With out Interruptio
                    Inscription of Sennacherib.

:* Reign of Esarhaddon . c . 681 - 669 . B . C .

42 History of phoenician City of
Sidon From Bronze age to Roman. **Sidon.** From page 41 . 41 صيدا مدينة

* prisoners from relief at Ninevh c.1853
* Stel fragment from Sidon (c. 850-750. B.C. Louve Museum paris)
* Reign of Nebuchadnesser II لهما مدينة
* Sidon become part of the Achaemenid prerian Empire c.599BC 539.B.
* Lion statuett dating to Achaemenid period 500 B.C. Louver. paris.
* Alexander the Great taken Sidon 332.B.C. صيدون الاسكندر احتل فيها
* During the Helenis Era Sidon Ruled By Both Talamic & Soloket Colocet Dynast.

* Relief from the Alexander Sarcophus
* Statue from Roman Sidon (c. 25; Louver Museum paris
11:04. Mon. Oct.10.2022 J.E.B. ف و ت   . ج . ل . ب

سلامات كوبان
c.363 -2800 **DILMUN** دلمون Civilisation
<u>Dilmun the Sumarian</u> Shanri-La (Bronz Age
Dilmun دلمون Civilization of Ancint Bahrain بحرين.
* Ruin of the Dilmun Civilization in Modern Bahrain بحرين.
* The famous **Adda Seal** c.2300 British. Museum London
* Cylinder Seal impression depicting the god Enki on his throne
  C. 225 B.C. Britsh. Museum London.

✓ The land Dilmun is holy, the land Dilmun is pure the land
  Dilmun is Clean Who had Lain by himself in Dilmun The place
  after Enki had Lain with his Wife That place is Clean that place
  is most bright... in Dilmun the raven Utters no Cry. The wolf Snatches
  not Lomb, Unkown is kid-devouring Wild dog, Unkown is grain-
  devouring boar The Sik-eye Says not "I am Sik-Eyed, The Sik-headed
  say not" I Sik-headed --- Its old man Say not" I am an old man
  "By the Side of the City he Utters no lament"
* Cylinder Seal impression with a possible depiction of Ziusudra
  (C. 3000-2300 B.C. Museum philadelphia U.S.A.)
* Relif of Ur Nanshe king of Lagash 2500 B.C. Louver. paris.

نبذة مختصرة دلمون DILMUN ق.م 363 - 2500 B.C.

ق.م 363 - 2800 Dilmun. From page. 42 ع٥ الكصيون

* Cylinder Seal Impression from Dilmun founder at Ur
(c. 2500 B.C. British Museum. London

* A'ali burial mound in Bahrain
(photo Courtesy of Bahrain Authority for Culture & Antiquities)

* Stamp Seal from Dilmun depicting hunters and goats
(c. 1500 B.C. Metropolitan of Art. New York U.S.A.

* Main Island of Dilmun Civilization (c. 2000-1000 B.C)

* Stamp Seal from Dilmun c. 2000-1500 Bahrain Museum

* Copper bull's Head found in the Ruin of Temple at Barbar
c. 2000 B.C. National Museum of Bahrin, Manama) معنى جربين

* Kassite Seal Impression with name of Uballissu-Marduk
(c. 1400 B.C Trutdes of the Britis Museum London (مروك

* Around 1220 B.C Tukti-Ninutal-I- of Assyrian Conqured Babylonia
and Land to Dilmun دعوة

"Mighty king king of Assyria and.
king of kardunaish Babylonia.
king of Sumer and Akkad.
king of Sippa and Babylonia.
king of Dilmun and Meluhha.
king of Upper and Lower Seas.
              Inscription of Tukti-Ninurta. 1.

* Stemp Seal from Dilmun
(c. 2000-1500. B.C.E.

2:00 Am.
     Tue.
         Oct. 11-2022.
                    ل.إ.د
                    ك. ف. ع. ب

Joseph. Bahr Bet

جوزيف. ابو فريحة كويتي

THE HISTORY OF ALPHABET

J.E.B.

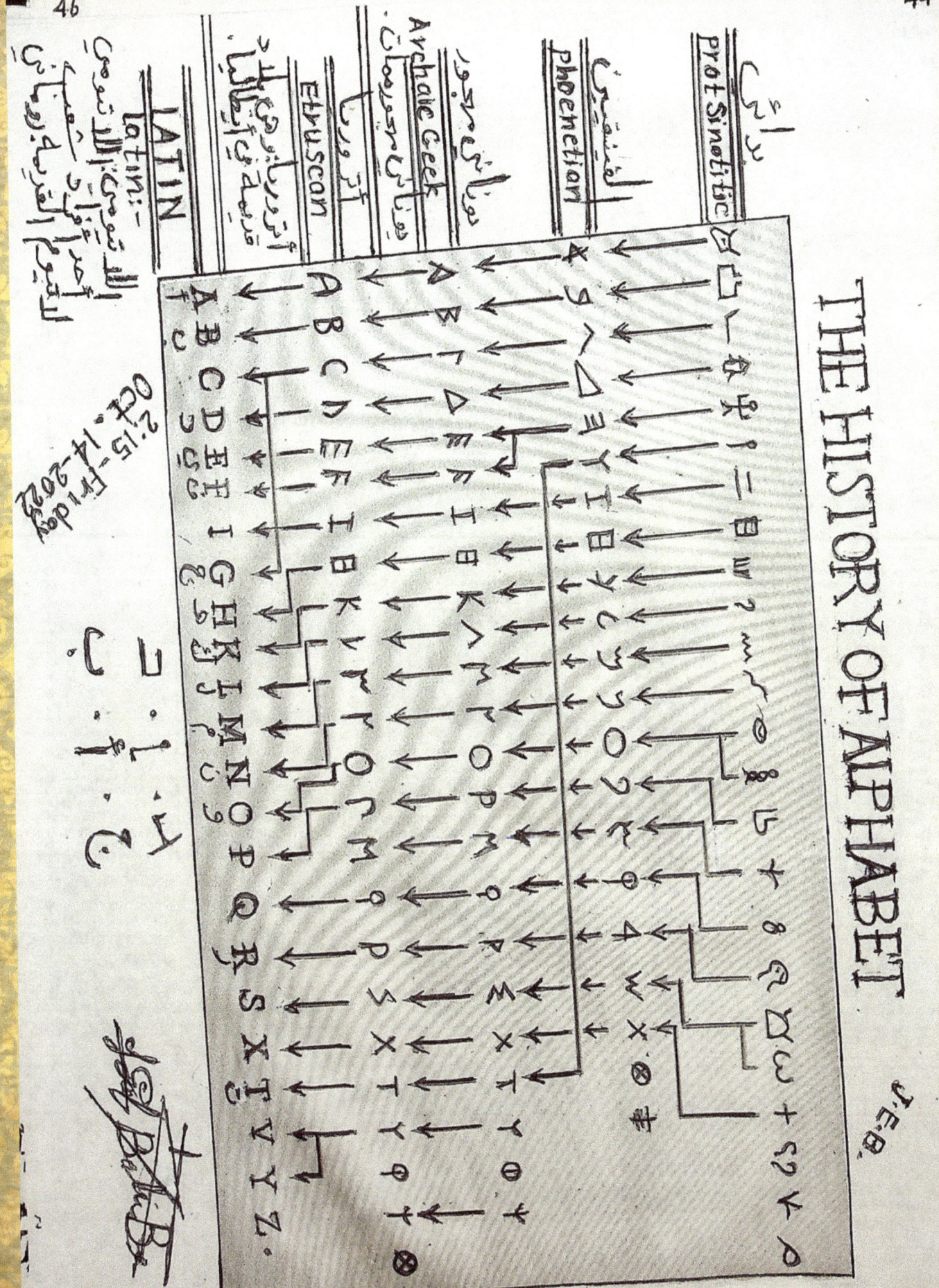

prot·Sinaitic	Phoenetian	Archaic Greek	Etruscan	LATIN
سلام أول	الفينيقية	اليونانية القديمة	الاتروسكانية	لاتيني

Oct. 14·Friday·2022
O:15

ABC

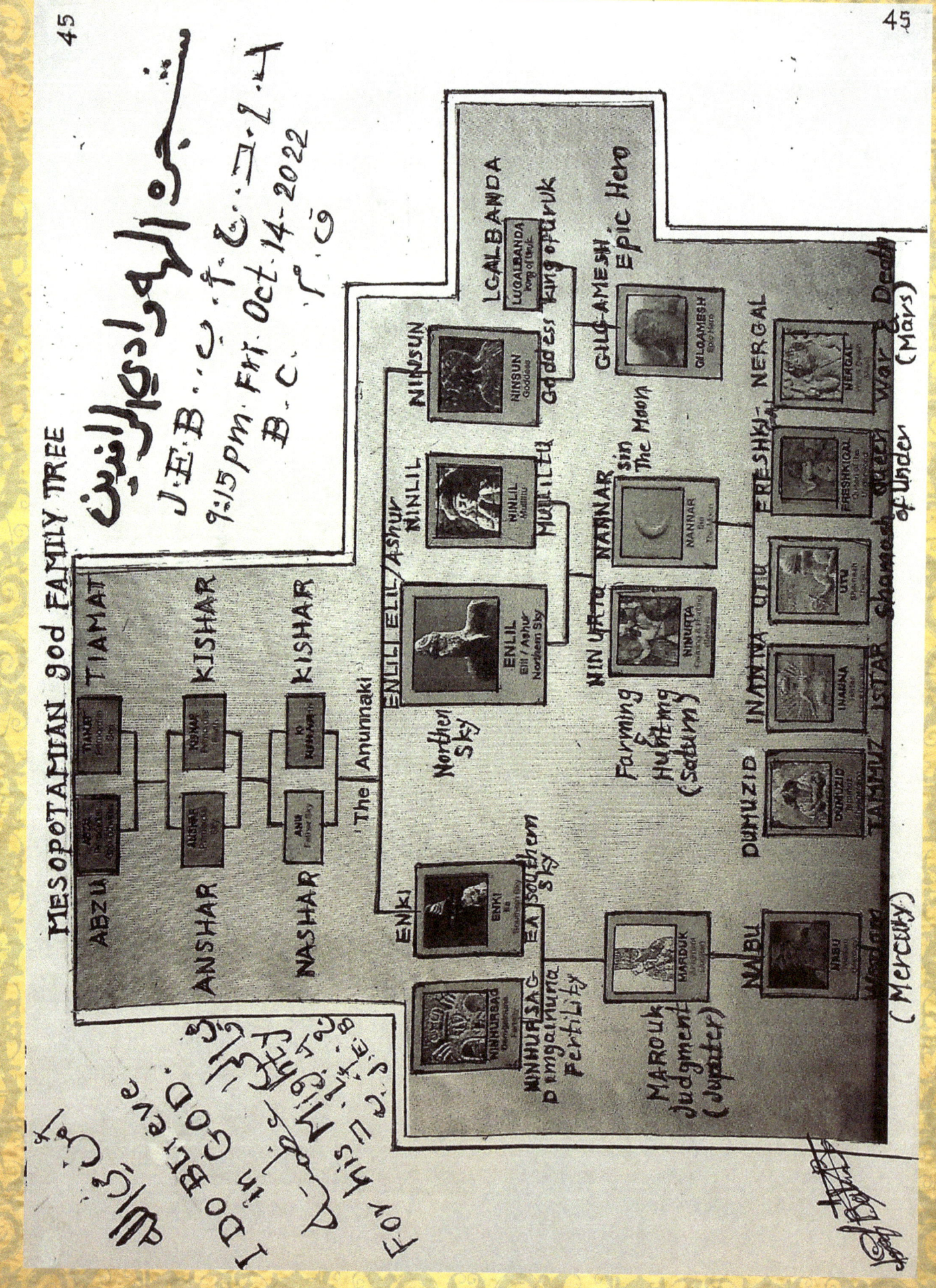

تطور الأحرف ألف وياء من الحاص الى الأحرف اللاتينيه

EVOLUTION OF THE ALPHABET

FROM ITS EARLIEST FORMS TO THE MODERN LATIN SCRIPT

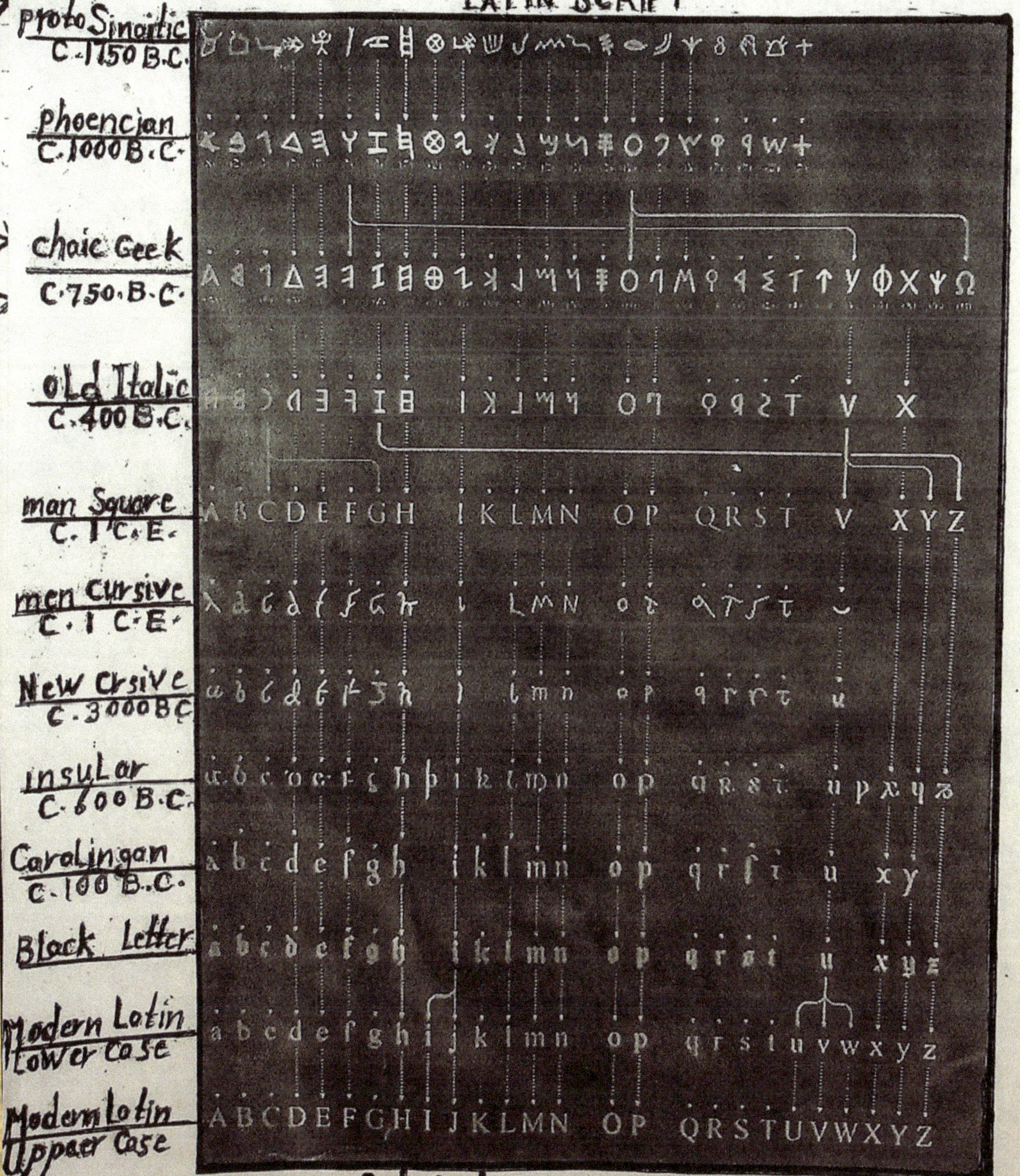

J.E.B.

Row labels (left side):

- proto Sinaitic C. 1750 B.C.
- phoencian C. 1000 B.C.
- chaic Geek C. 750. B.C.
- Old Italic C. 400 B.C.
- man Square C. 1 C.E.
- men Cursive C. 1 C.E.
- New Crsive C. 300 B.C.
- insular C. 600 B.C.
- Carolingan C. 100 B.C.
- Black Letter
- Modern Latin Lower Case
- Modern Latin Uppaer Case

4:55 pm Sat. Oct. 15 - 2022 J.E.B.

Anciant Greece

Ancient Greece
* Peloponnee — South wes pennsula
* Attica — Southwes pennsula
* Boetia — Central Greece
* Thessaly — Originally Acalia
* Minoan's — C. 3500-1100 B·C·

Maccanion part Indo Eurpin Emgration the Name Come
From Maycediny Macedona is part Indo Eurpian Lengege Immigra-
tion
Emmigration & Family Indo Eurpian - Iranian & prisia
This grup Immigrated From North Aruond 900·C· to West
Eurpe· My Cantact With Minoanian.
* Mycenaean Age C· 1750-105 B·C·
* Greek Dark Ages C· 1050-750 B·C·
* HEROES OF THE TROIAN WAR
* ARETE Exellence or realization of potensial
For Aruond 800 B·C· Greeks Experence to Structure
Revoletion With Small Vilges Became Small Indepnte

* Hoplites (the Army man) (the Ancient Greek)

Greek
shiela
Called
hoplon
shield & hoplon
← Bronze breas plate
Hoplites
Long pears
doru.
in right hand

* Arstcras, Arstcracy & Democracy
* Sparta
* Athens
* Lycurgus Semi-Legendary Lawgiver (·820-730·B·C·
* Spartiates
* peloponneisen Leage C·550-366 B·C·

Ancient Geek

* **Solon**: Athenion archon & lawgiver   C. 630 - 560 B.C.
  1 - Lond debts Cancelled. 2 - Freed slaves. 3 - Banned loans with human Collatera

* **Cleisthenes**: Father of Athenian democrary   C. 570 - 508 B.C.

Demoskratas   Demos kratos

Demos   kratos
common people; jistset   rule; strengh

* **Marathon**   Demdkrata
* **Storm off Euboeu**   Greek
  destroys large   papuler government
  poortion of   democratia
  perisan fleet   Medieval latin
* **Battle of   democrtia
  Solamis 4800 B.C.**   MedLe Franch
* **Battle of plataes 479 B.C.**   * Age of pericles 461-429 Bc
* **Pericles. 495 - 429 - B.C.**
* **Great peloponnsian War 431 - 404 B.C.**
* **Herodotus Fathe of History 484 - 425 B.C.**
* **Aeshy Lus. Father of Trcgedy 525 - 456 B.C.**
* **Aristophones Master of old Comedy 446 - 386 B.C.**
* **Socrates Creek philosophy 470 - 399 B.C.**
* **Aristotle Geek philosopher 394. 322. B.C.**

Aristotle Form gavemment
The true Constitution aim the Common Good

Royalty	Aristocracy	Constitutional Government
Tyanny (A)	Oliaarchy (B)	Democracy (C)

the peverted Constitutions aim For the Well of a
part of City (the tyrant; the Wealth of the indigent).

Aristotle is a
So it is naturaly With Male & the female the
one is Superior, the other
governer the Other is govern red, & the Same
rule must necesirily hold good with respect to
AL mankind   Aristotle

*Aristotle is a Hellenistic
ALexsander is Macedonian

Women are Unfinished men
- ((Ar Stotle)) -
Aristotle Free the Slavery women

*Hercules
Wolls
With the
Buddha

*ptolemuia
Dynasty
Egypt
*Arinoe II
Queen of
ptolemaic
Egypt
273-268 B.C

*Eratash-
enes of
Cyrene:-
Father of
Geography
276-194 B.C
* Euclid
Father of
Geomtry
Active-300 B

*Panhellenic Games. The four differen Locations
1- Olympia. 2- Delphi. 3- Isthmia. 4- Nemea
*Antigonid Dynasty. Macedonia and Greek City & States
*Aristarchus of Samos. Heliontric Model 310-230 B.C
*Archimedes: Mathematicn engeneer Inventor Astronomer
1:05 Am. Fri. Oct. 15-2022. J. E. B ⊐ ⌐ ⌐ Physicist. 297-212. B.C

ISAIA: 19:25-26 إشعياء

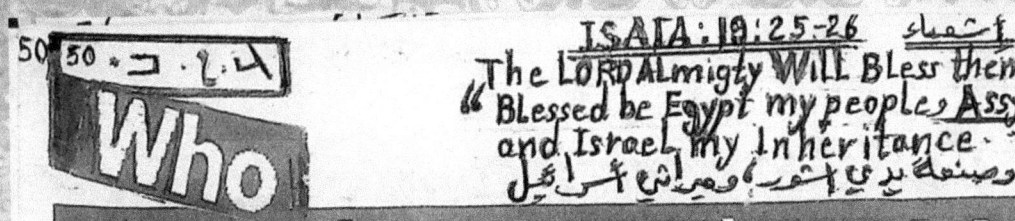

The LORD Almigty WILL Bless them Saying,
" Blessed be Egypt my people, Assyria my Hand Work and Israel my Inheritance.

فيباركهم الرب القدير قائلا
مبارك ربا شعبي مصر وصنعة يدي آشور وميراثي إسرائيل

Who were the Assyrians? History

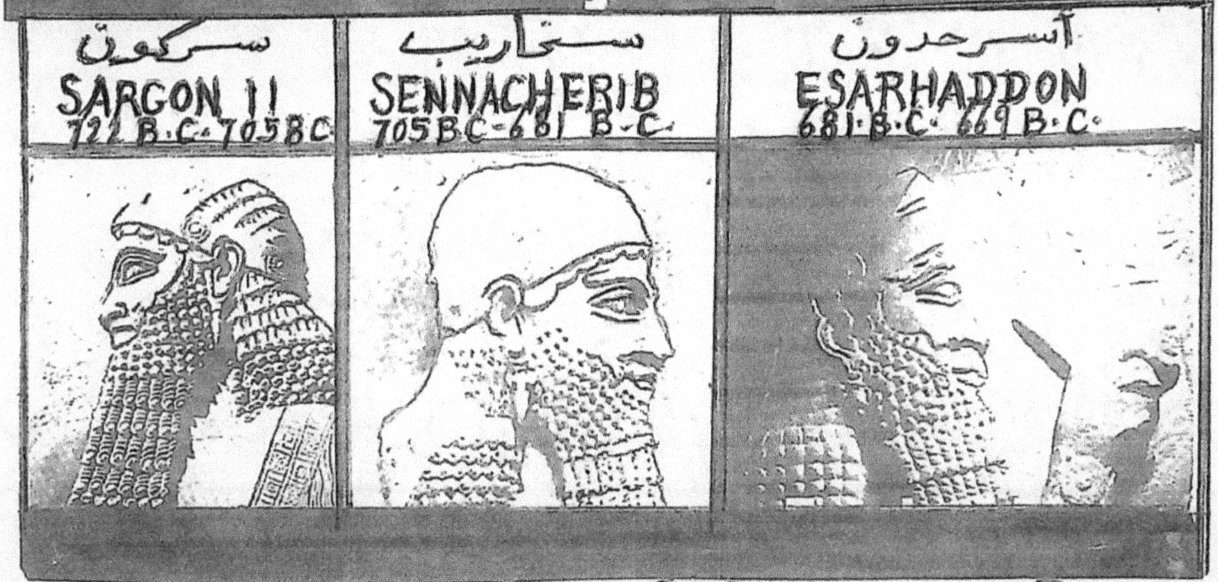

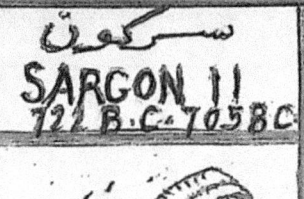

سركون
SARGON II
721 B.C. 705 B.C.
سنحاريب
SENNACHERIB
705 B.C. 681 B.C.
أسرحدون
ESARHADDON
681 B.C. 669 B.C.

NOV. 21 2022

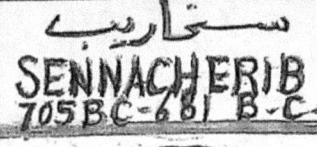

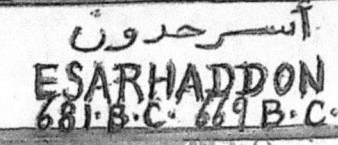

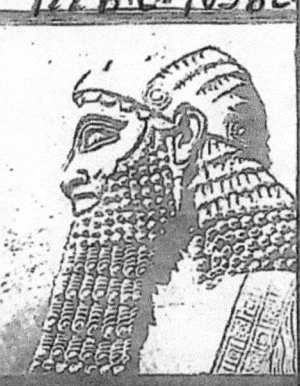

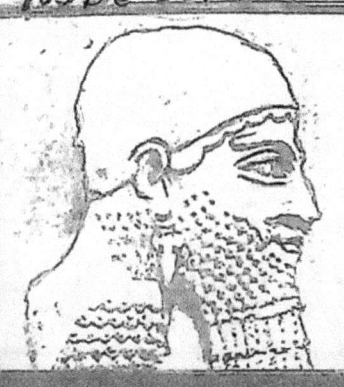

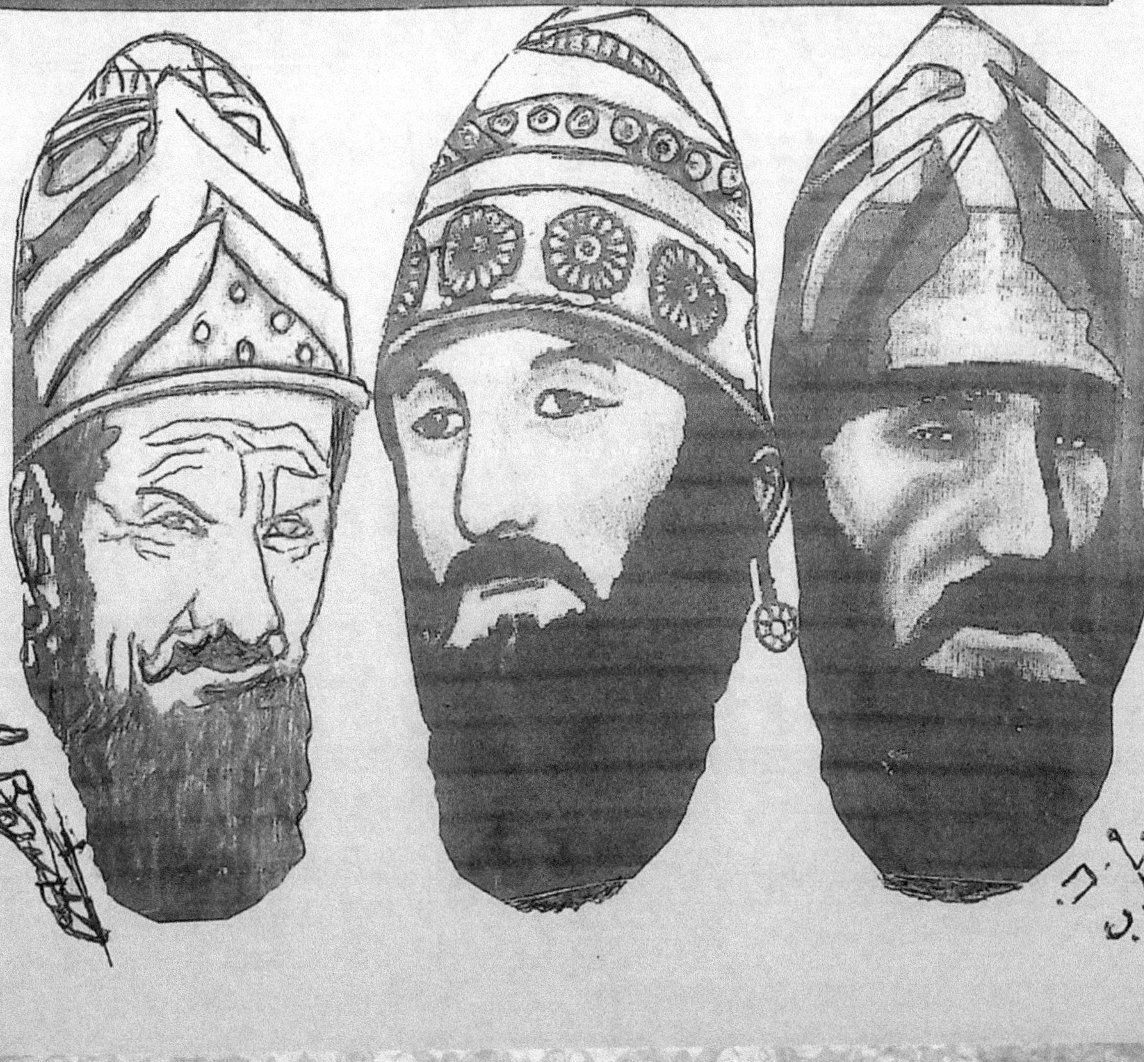

Neo-Assyrian kings

1- Shalmaneser, III 858-824. B.C.E.
2- Shamshi-Adad V. 823-811. B.C.E.
3- Adad-Nirari. III. 810-783. B.C.E.
4- Shalmaneser. IV. 782-773. B.C.E.
5- Ashur-dan. III. 772-755. B.C.E.
6- Ashur-nirari. V. 754-746. B.C.E.
7- Tiglat-pileser. III. 745-727. B.C.E.
8- Shalmaneser. V. 726-722. B.C.E.
9- Sargon. II. 721-705. B.C.E.
10- Sennacherib 704-681. B.C.E.
11- Esarhaddon 680-669. B.C.E.
12- Ashurbanipal 668-630 B.C.E.

Omiaede Dynasty of Israel

1- Omri   885-874   B.C.E.
2- Ahab   874-853. B.C.E.
3- Ahaziah   853-852. B.C.E
4- Jehoram   852-841. B.C.E

Jehu Dynasty of Israel

1- Jehu   841-814. B.C.E
2- Jehoahaz   814-798. B.C.E
3- Jehoash   798-782. B.C.E
4- Jeroboam II   793-753. B.C.E
5- Zechariah   753-752. B.C.E.

ٮ ﻑ ٤   J.E.B   ﻥ ٤ ﻝ

Sep. 2022.

Ancient ASSYRIN at War.

* Neo-Assyrian Empire during reign of Assurbanipal
* Bronze plaque from door c. 850 B.C. (Louvre Museum paris)
* Cylinder Seal Impression From the Area Around Ashur c 2500 B.C. (Louver paris)
* Meopotimia and the Levat (c. 2000-1800 B.C.
* Broken Stela of Naram-Sin c. 2254-2218 B.C. Archaeological Museum Istanbul
* Tablel from thign of Shulg of Ur Uncoved in Nineveh c. 2094-2074 B.C. Louver paris.
* Broken Stela of Shamshi-Adad c. 1767-1775, Louver Museum paris
* c. 1792-1750 B.C. Votive plagu of Hammurabi of Babylon British London
* Hithite invasion of Babylonia (c. 1595 B.C.)
* Mitanni لَتا نيِ Cylinder Seal impressions 15th Century New York.
* Mitanni لَتا Control of Ashur much of Northern Mesopotamia 15th century B.C
* Tablet From Mari (c1780B.C. Louver paris
* Headless Assyrian Statue Louver Museum paris. c. 1400-1000 B.C
* Assyrian Sikle Sword c. 1307-1275 Museum of Art, New York City
* Midle Assyrian Text. c. 1350 B.C. British Museum London
* Relief From the Palace of Ashur banipl. c. 668-630 B.C. British Museum London)
* Neo-Assyrian Empire during the Reign of Ashur banipal. c. 650-630 B.C.
* Drawing of Wall relief From Nineveh c. 1850 B.C.
* Relief from the palace of Sennacherib c. 704-681 B.C. British London
* Relief of an Archer c. 710 B.C. Louver paris.
* Relief depicting Tiglath-pilese III dignitriaries. 745-727 B.C. Detroit U.S.A.
* Relief of light infantry Soldiers c. 668 B.C. British London
* Drawing of Soldiers found on reliefs from Nineveh. 1853 B.C.
* Portrait of two Assyrian Soldiers 650 B.C. Louver paris
* Relief of An Assyrian Soldiers scaling the Walls of Elamite fortes 640 B.C. British London
* Assyrian Cavalry
* Soldiers 700 B.C. British London. * Assyrian Cavolry officer 650 B.C.
* Relief depicting an Assyrian Chariot off into Battle 710 B.C. paris
* Relief depicting Light infantry an noncombtants 650 B.C. London
* procession depicting Ashurbanibal II. 883-859 B.C. London.

3:43 pm MON Oct 17 2022 J.E.B. أبو بكر

Mayans LL

Entire History the Mayans
Spanish Empler
1490 - 1976

* Diego Garcia de polacio Spanish Colonial Offical (16th.C)
* Sir Francis Drake English naval officer, explore & politicyan
* philip-11- king of Spain (1556-1598)   1540-1596

CLASSIC MAYA CIVILIZATION 300-900AD

EARLY MIDDLE AGES C. 476-1000
* Chorlemagne شارل king of Frank (768-814)

CALAKMUE
PRE-CLASSIC MAYA 1000 B.C - 250 A.D.
* Francisco Hernandez de Cordoba spanish Conquistador Early 16 Century
* Herman Cortes Spanish & Conquistador & Conquerer of Aztec
* Fransisco pizarro Spanish   Empir 1485-1547
Conquistador & Conqueror of Inca Empir.
* Bernal Diaz del Castilo Spanish Congictador &
          Chronicler 1492-1584

SPANISH EXPEDITION TO YUCATON 1518
* JUAN De Grijalva Spanis Conquistador 1490- 1527
✓ AZTEC EMPIR 1428 - 1521
Nachi Cacom Maya War leader Mid.16.Century)

* John Llayl Stephens U.S.A Explorer Writer & diplomat 1805-1862
* Jean- Frederic de Waleck Franch antiqurian Explorer 1786-1875
✓ EL MIRADOR: large Templ Ancian Maya
✓ EL TIGRE Complex (Temple).
✓ LA DATA PYRAMID Temple
✓ TEOTIHUACAN Central Mexico Temple of Sun
TERMINAL PRE -CLASSIC C. 100-250 A.D.
TIKAI

From paeg 53 ٥٣ صفحة من يابا Maya كتمل

* Diego De landa
  Spanish Fransiscan Bishop 1524-1579
- Relacion de las Cosas de lacon
  Book by Digo De Landa 1566
- Incidents of Travel in Central America, Chiapon and
  Yucon   Book by John Lloyd Stephen 1843
  Jean-Francois Champollion Transletor of Egyption
  Writing System 1790-1832
* Stephens & CatherWood American & British Eplores Mid 19th.C
* Chilam Balam Maya Book 17th-18th. Century
* Ernst Forsteman German Historion 1822-1906
* Joseph Goodman American. Weiter 1838-1917
* Eduard Seler German Anthrapologist & Lingist 1849-1922
* Tatiana proskouria koff Russian-American Archaelogist 1909-1985
✓ LINER.B. Old World Greek SYLLABIC SCRIT
* pacal the Great king of Palenque 615-683
✓ AZTEC EMPIR 1428-1521 الأمبروطوريه لأزتكه
✓ OLMEC CULTUR c.1600-400.B.C.
  Red palace San Lorenzo
✓ PRE-CLASSIC MESOAMERICA. c 2500-250 A.D
  PRE-CLASSIC MAYA C.1000 B.C-250 A.D.
  MIDDLE PRE-CLASSIC MAYA. c.1000 400 B.C
* Ambrosio Tut Governer of peten 19th. Century
  AZTEC EMPIR 1428-1521 أمبروطوريه الأزتكه
✓ Sihyai Chan K'awiil.II. Ajaw of Tikal. 411-456
* Morzillo Hernan Cartes horse
* Father Fuenesalida Spansh priest Early 17th. Century
  ATZA Maya people
  CHICHEN ITZA 750-1200 A.D.
* Pedro de Alvardo the Cruel Spanish Conquisador & Coverner of Gutemala 1485-1541
45 Am. MON. Oct-17-2022. J.B. كتابه وتدوين في اليوم التاني

Maya LL.   From page 54. دير ين Maya دارك

MAYAPAN c 1000-1461

TAYSAL

ULATLAN K'ICHE' CAPITAL

Tecun Uman k'iche War Leader (1500-1524)

K'ICHE MAYA PEOPLE

Ximenez Spanish Churchmon 18th Century

Popol Vuh Mythology and history of K'ich people 16th, C

Chilam Balam Series of Maya Books 17th-18th Century

Rabinal Achi Maya Theatrcal play

Hunahpu & Xbalangue Maya Hero Twins Creation Story

Hun Huahpu Maize God in Mayan Mythology

POSE CLASSIC MAYA c.900-1500

~ VIII END OF AN AGE.

✗ Chirstopher Columbus Italian explorer & Firt governor of
Indies 1451-1506

✗ Juan de Grijalva Spanish Chonquistador 1490-1527

Juan Diaz Chroicler & Chaplain of the 1518 De Grijalva Expedition

TULUM

COBA

CHICHEN TZA

TERMINAL·CLASSIC·PERIOD c.800-1000 A.D.

CLASSIC MAYA COLLAPSE C 9th-11th C.A.D

TIKAL   CALAKMUL· UXMAL UXMAL SAYIL

TERMINAL CLASSIC PERIOD c.800-1000 A.D

POST CLASSIC 900-1500·A.D.

CHEN ITZA c.750-1200 A.D.

TOLEC INVASION HYPOTHESIS 100-1000 A.D

Quetzelcoatl popular MesoaAmerican Daily

JAINA STATU

✗ MAYAPAN c-1000- 1441.·✗ 1491-America Befor Columbus

✗ Canek Maya Rebel Leader 18 Century

Spanish Empir 1492-1976

From page 39

ارة ميز دارك
TUE-OCT-18-2021
J-E-B.
U.T.E.

Cush ETHIOPIA Hbashah
كوش حبشة

3000 years Ethiopia ((cush)) History

cush Son of Ham
كوش بن حام

D'mt
Da'amat or Da'mat
1000 B.C - 400 B.C

* The Ethiopia church Mantain Ark Covenent in the chapal

Egypt (مصر)

Red Sea

كوش kush Nubia

D'MT

Axumite Himyar Saba

* Great power Rais Early Aksum (Axum)
100 B.C - 100 AD

* Mani. 216AD-274AD

* king - Ezana
320 AD - 360 AD
Converet to Christianity

* Obilisk of Ezana

✓ kinadom of kush 785 B.C - 350 A.D.   كوش مملكة

✓ Axumite Empire 520AD - 525 A.D.

✓ kingdom of ALODIA

✓ Yodit Appox 960 - 1000

✓ Mara Takla Haymanot 1137 - 1270

✓ Zeawe dynasty 1137 - 1270

✓ Ruler of Zegwe dynasty Gebre Mesqel lalibela 1181 - 1221. Constructed 11 Churches

* Yekuno Amlak 1270 - 1285

✓ ABYSSIN / ADAL SULTANATE

✓ Abyssinian حبشي - Adal War 1529 - 1543

✓ Dawit II. 1507 - 1540

Age of princes Zemene Mesafint 1769 - 1955

57

Continue Ethiopia

كمله أثوبيا   From page 56   من صفحة   Ethiopia كلاد

* Tewodros II 1855-1868
✓ British Expedition to Abassina 1867-1868
* Ismail posha 1863-1879 of Egypt Invet Ethiopia
* Yohannes IV 1871-1889
✓ Ethiopian Egyptian war 1874-1876
* Menelik II   1889-1913
✓ First Italo-Ethiopian war 1894-1896
✓ Second Italo-Ethiopian war 1935-1939
✓ Italian East Africa 1936-1941
* Haile Selassie Reign 193-1974
✓ Provisional Militry Government Socialist Ethiopia
  or DERG for short 1974-1987
* Mengistu Haile Marjam
✓ people Democratic Republic of Ethiopia (cush)
      1787-1999
  Transitional Government of Ethiopia منتقله
      1991-1995

* (Cush)   Ethiopia (Hbashah)

    1995-present day

8:50 pm. Oct.18-2022. اب. اكتوبر. ١٨
      J.E.B.
   * Cush Son of Ham Son of Noah
    كوش أبن حام أبن نوح

Babylonian

The first Babylonian Dynasty Anant Mesopotamia Hammurabi
The Study of Antiquit & the Middle Ages
PRESENTS
Hammurabi
AND THE
First Dynasty of Babylonia

The Sumerian king List is one the Oldes Such docments in Mesopotamian and Word history. It Serves As an offical Canon of Sumerian history Starting from when king Ship Was bestowed Unto Sumer from Heavn, Supposedly abut 250,000 yeas ago.

This kingship was initially heldat the City of Eridu befor a Great flood, but then moved to Varios Other Cities, It Was generly held by Most poweful City in Sumer, thus Creating a Series of dynasties ruling Over the regen.

1924 B.C.
✓ King List Dynasty :
* Isin : Ur-Ninurta
✓ Other Attested Dynasty
* Larsa : Gunguhum.
✓ 1816 B.C.
king List Dynasty
* Isin : Sinmagir
✓ Other Attested Dynasty
* Larsa: Rim-Sin
Around 1763 B.C the Last independent Sumerian kingdom Larsa was Coptured by Amorites king of Babylon Hammurabi, The king List doesn make referenc to any dynasty after this point

Continue Babylon . . Babylonian J.L. from page 58 اسم الله

Babylon clay tablet YBC 7289 with annotations The diagonal display an approximi ation of the Square root of 2 in for Sexgesimal figures, 1 24 51 10, Which is good to abut Six decimal digits.

The Babylonian System of mathematics, Was a Sexagesimal ((base 60 numeral System From this We derive the Modren day Usago of 60 Seconds in a minute, 60 minutes in an hous, and 360 degrees in Circle

The Ancint Sumerian of Mesopotamia developed a Complex System of metrology From 3000 B.C.
From 2600 B.C. onwards the Sumerians Wrote multiplication tablet on Clay tablets and dealt With geometrical exercises and divion problems The earliest traces of Babylonian numerals Also date back to this period.

Wed. Oct. 19-2022

J. E. B.

Always I praiset
the mighty Lord
I Love him So much
I Believe in him
God. Jesus.
J. E. B.
Holy Spirit
Amen
X

SEMIRAMIS AND THE ANCIENT INDIANS

SEMIRAMIS ((Shmiram)) & the Ancient India سميراس

كلا يقولون ويعتقدون أن

Biblical Shem = king Bharat of India ملك براتِ أن

((Father of ALL Samites)) من هنا جاب هو أمين

((Manu, Brahma, Satya Uradha, Rishabha Nata))

Noah

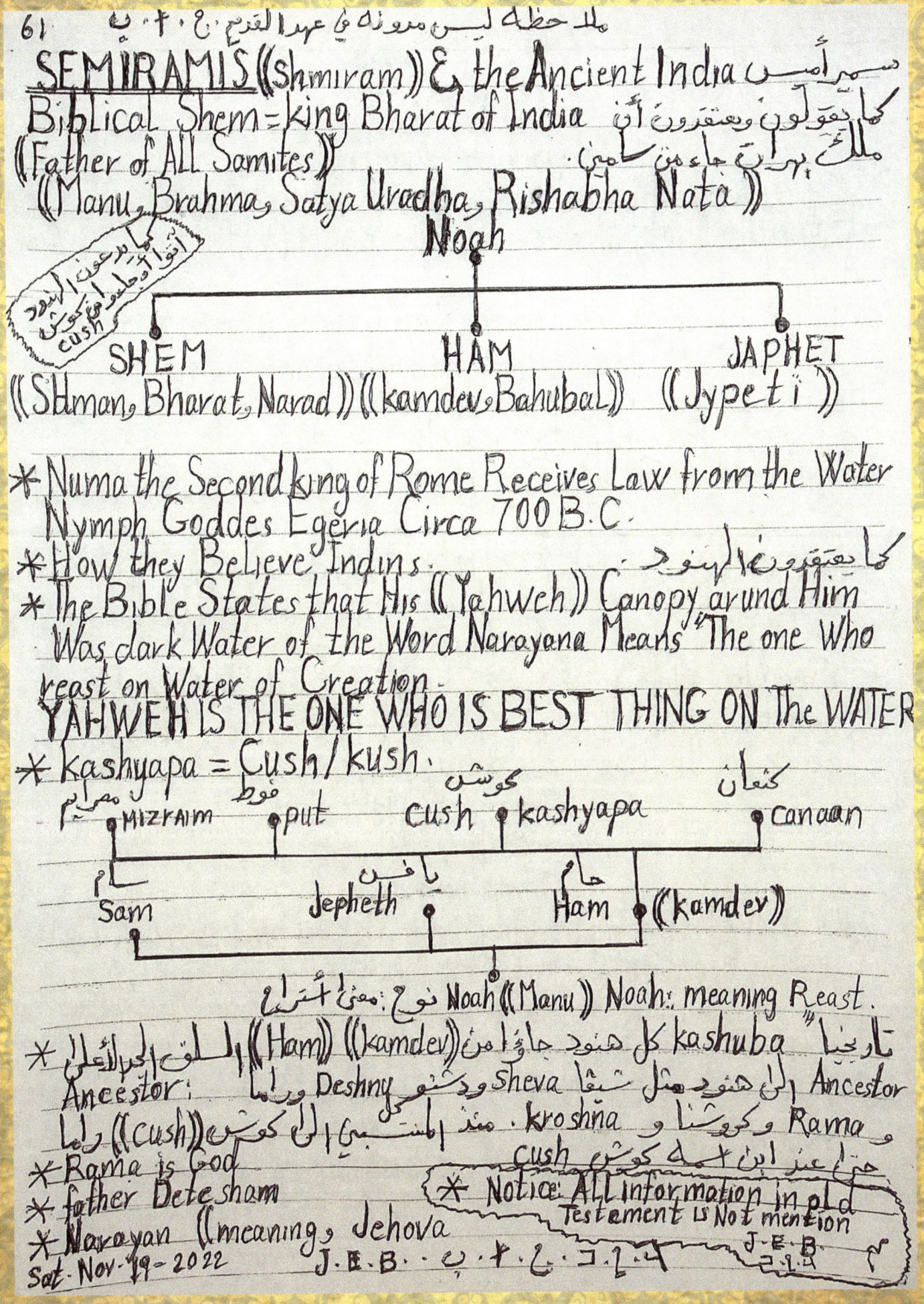

انقوا بدعون السوء واطلبوا توبتوا cush

SHEM **HAM** **JAPHET**

((Shman, Bharat, Narad)) ((kamdev, Bahubal)) ((Jypeti))

---

* Numa the Second king of Rome Receives Law from the Water
  Nymph Goddes Egeria Circa 700 B.C.
* <u>How they Believe</u> Indins. كما يعتقدون الهنود
* The Bible States that His ((Yahweh)) Canopy around Him
  Was dark Water of the Word Narayana Means The one Who
  reast on Water of Creation.

YAHWEH IS THE ONE WHO IS BEST THING ON The WATER

* Kashyapa = Cush/kush.

مصرم MIZRAIM   فوط put   حوش CUSH ⋅ kashyapa   كنعان canaan

يافث Sam   Jepheth   حام Ham ⋅ ((kamdev))

نوح معنى أستراح Noah ((Manu)) Noah: meaning Reast.

* تاريخنا kashuba كل هنود جاء من ((Ham)) ((kamdev)) الاقى الأعلى
  Ancestor: إلى هنود من هنا Sheva شيفا و Deshny ديشنو و Ancestor
  إلى ((Cush)) كوش إلى يسمانا اللى عبان Rama و كوشنا krashna
* Rama is God
* father Dete sham
* Narayan ((meaning Jehova
  cush كوش ⋅ و إبن إسراع

* Notice: ALL information in old
  Testament is Not mention

كهلائم

NIMROD
Biblical Archaeologe

* Who was Nimrod? He Come from Cush
Ethopia (Habbsha حبشة) He was Mighty Man Hunter
After GOD Gen.
and his kingdom began in Shinar
        Babel. Uruk Akkad Calaeh   بابل. أوروك. أكد
and he Conquered Assyrian Region
Nineveh. Rehobth. Ir. Calah.   Resen
* The Sons of CUSH: Seb Havilah Sabtah Raamah and
Sabteca   Genesis: 10:7
* SARGON of AKKAD From KISH
* Salma the father of Bethlam and Hareph the father
of Beth-gader. 1. Chronicales 2:5
* See Also Nubers. 21:25. 2king 16:17. CUSH Could be
Siad to be the father of KISH like Salma was the
father of the town of Bethlehem
        Sargon of Akkad
        سرجون الأكدي
        Thron Neme
We know littel abut Sargon of Akkad himself He is real
name is Unown: Sarru-kin (sic) meaning the true
king in Akkadian is abviously a thron nam
* Nimrod king the kish of Sumer & Akkad etus testamentuin   Vol 52
* Nimrod Indentifing Nimrod of Genesis 10. With Sargon Akkad
* Calneh that is Nofer Ninefi City of Nippur
* The Begining of his kingdom was babel. Erech Akked and
Calneh in the Land of Shinar شنعار Gen:10.10
* Hamnurabi III GAL MARDU king of the Amorites))

Queen Sheb

King Solomon عليه السلام reigned after the Death of King Daivd, عليه السلام. Following King David's Death the people of Israel began Scrificing on the high places. a pagan practice Learned from thier Canaanite neighbors that Violated Mosic Law Despite his pagan practices Solomon Loved the Lord by Walking in his Father Daivd's footseps. He was a Gibeon which Was the most famous high place that Solomon famously asked the Lord for Wisdom God began the procedings by Appearing to Solomon & making an incredible offer he was Wise Beyond his years When he became king he was abut 20 yers old The young man Was aware of his Shortcomings He had no prior Leader- ship experience but he been appinted ruler of Large a Number of people What he required a receptive heart in Order to judg and Lead them Correctly Realizing your desp- erate need for God is the first Step toward becoming a kingdom man God Was So pleased that Solomon requested Wisdom rather than, Long Life or riches that He granted the requst & then added What Solomon did not request riches honor & a long life However in Order for thses promised blessing to bccom a reality Solomon have to Walk in the ways of the Lord & follow his Statutes & commands God's promises Were Certin but they coud only be Obtaind through Obedience Solomons reaction to the encounter was Worship & feasting Solomon became What Would Call renissance man As a result of Gods plessing there Was no Subject of what he did not possess Unrivaled Wisdom He Was a proverbial Author a Song Composer & even a botdist & Zoologist 1. king: 4:32 and 33 . And he Speak of trees from the Cedar tree that is in Lebanon even Unto the hyssop

that springeth out of the wall. He speak also of beasts &
a foul & of creeping things & of fishes His Wisdom for Supassed
that of ALL the peoples of the east & all of Egypts Wisdom was
Sinificant because these regions were renowned for their
Wisdom in fact the author of kings stated Unequivocally that
there was no comparison Solomon was Wiser than anyone
Furthermore Solomons reputation was well-known the
Surrounding nations came to know and rsepect Isreals king
Every king on the plant dispatched emissraries to hear
Solomons Wisdom Gods kingdom was blessing the kingdom
of the World 1: king 4:29-34 God gave Solomon Wis-
dom & great discernmt. His insghts were as Numerous as
Sand on the Sea shore Solomon was Wiser than any of
the Eastern Leaders & Wiser than anyone in Egypt
Wiser than Ethan the Ezrahit, Heman. & Wiser than Mahols
Sons Chalcol & Dards Hs reputainiton was know throughout
the Surrounding nations Solomon Wrot 3000 provebs &
1005 Song' He described trees evrey things from Ceders
that grow in Lebanon to hyssop that grow on garden wall
He described animals birds reptiles & fish people Came
from every Where to hear Solomons advice Every king on
the earth hear of his Wisdom It was typical of king to
Send emissaries to Solomon However this Queen Came
herself to Confirm the word That She heard
We previously learned that Solomons fame had Spread
Widely the Story of Queen of SHEBA exemplifies this
point It also demonstrates that God was plessing
the worlds peoples through his people Just as had
promised Abraham Genesis: 12:3 And I will bless the
that bless thee And in these shall all families of the Earth
be blessed.

From page 64 عن Sheba 65
continue From page

The Queen of SHEBA paid a Visit to Solomos Court

ﺑﻘﻴﺔ ﻗﺼﺔ ﺍﻟﻤﻠﻜﺔ ﻭﺍﻟﻤﻠﻚ ﺳﻠﻴﻤﺎﻥ She Was From an Arabian kingdom & What is now Yemen ﺍﻟﻴﻤﻦ Her Country was about 1200 miles ﻣﻴﻞ From Jerusalem The Queen Came to See Solomon because of his fame associted With the name of Lord which Was most Likely a reference to the wisdom that the Lord had bestowed Upon him. She Come to put him to the test with riddles to See if his abilities Lived Up to his reputation 1 kings 10:1. When the Queen of Sheba heard abut the fame of Solomon & his relationship to the Lord She Came test Solomon with hard questions She Wasnt exactly a popper herself bringing a Large enturage of expensive and exotic gifts With her 1 King 10:2 Arriving at Jerusalem With a Very great Caravan, With Camels Carrying Spices Larg quantities of gold and precious stones about all that she had on her mind But Solomons Wisdom & Wealth Were far beyond her Comprhension It took her breath away by the time she had heard his explanation & Seen his glorious kindom 1. king 10:3-5 Solomon Answered all her question. Nothing was hard for the king to explain to her When the Queen of Sheba Saw all the wisdom of Solomon and the palace he had built the food of his table the Seating of his officials the attending Servants in their robes, his Cup bearer & the burnt offerings he made at the temple of the Lord She Was overwhelemed the Visiting Queen Admited she had not believed the reports abut Solomon that she had heard, but she'd Seen for her Self that he Was the real deal She then thanked the Lord for putting Solomon on the throne for the Sake of Irael 1 king 10:6-8 She Said to the king The report I herd in my own Country

<u>About your Achievements & your Wisdom is true</u> but I did
<u>not belivde these things Until I Came and Saw With my</u>
<u>own Eyes</u> Inded not even half Was told me in wisdom
& wealth you have for exceeded the report I heard How
happy your people must be How Happy you Officials
Who Continually Stand befor you & her you Wisdom she
also Lavished Solomon With gifts & he appers to have
reciprocated 1 king 10:9-13. praise be to the Lord
your God Who has dilghted in you & placed you on
the throne of Israel Becaus of the lords eternal Love
for Israel He has made you king to maintain Justice and
righteounes & She gave the king 120 talents of Gold
Large quntities of Spices & precious stones Never again
Were So many Spices brought in as those the Queen
of SHEBA gave Solomon Hiram Ships brought gold
from Ophir & from there they brought great Cargoes
almugwood & precious Stones the king Used the
almugwood to make Supports for temple of the Lord
& for the royal palace & to mak harps & Lyres for the
musicians. So much almugwood has never been Imprted
or Seen Since that day <u>king Solomon gave the Queen of</u>
<u>of Sheba all she desired & asked for besid What he had</u>
given her out of his Royal bounty Than She Left and
<u>returned With her Routine to her own Country</u> & inters-
ting insght into the Queen of SHEBA is that she did not
take people at face Value Whether that be on the has is
<u>of their Self-report or the reputation they had garnered</u> x
<u>from other peole in other Word she Wanted to see the results</u>
<u>for her Self</u> Anothe interesting thing the Queen Shepa demostrated or
<u>attempt to strike a Closer relationship With him Until she was s-</u>
<u>isfied that he deserved them</u>

From page 66 من صفحة Sheba تكمله مكتابه ا

Was that she did not share any of her gifts with Solomon
or attempt to strike a closer relationship with him
Until she was satisfied that he deserved them, later
Jesus mentioned the Queen of Sheba also called the
Queen of the South in His Conemnation of Scribes, & pharise
pharisees Matthew 12:42 the Queen Sheba of South

11:15 pm ‏١١، ١٥ دقيقه‏ أنتهيت من كتابه هذا الكتاب في الساعه
في اليوم الأثنين مصادف ١٠ / 31 - 2022

† Complete Writing this Book
On Monday. & October· 31 - 2022
On Saints Eve & Halloween Eve
Tim: 11:15 pm

تشرين الأول <·<<·> ع
Happy Saints Eve

Happy Hallow
J.E.B.

J·E·B

* Saints Eve. Changed to Witch· J.E.B
Changed Day or Eve·J.E.B
Crafts Day or Eve

Author and Usher· J.E.B

† I Do BeLive in GOD &
AL Saints
† I Do Believe in God &
Amen أمن
J.E.B

اللاد العربيه لن تتوقف ماعن العراق - سوى الحضرات القديمه

سومياً العراق بلاد ما بين النهرين وبيت النهرين في الأزمنه وموسوبوتاميا في اليونان ولفظ العراق يرجع من أصله إلى القرن اللغوي من العصور القديمه مشتق من كلمه أوروك أي العمق والى تعني مستوطنه العراق أول مستوطن أو المستوطنه الشبيه منذ بدأ الخلق ومن حديثها الذكر أن كلمه أوروك هي أساس الجذر الذي اشتق منها مدينه السومريه الوركا في البابليه في الكتب العرق ومعنى كلمه العرق أي العربيه هو أرضنا الداخل وقال أنه سبب تسميه هو تعريب الاخ من الي حيث أن كل أنقاء عند النهر أو النهرين العراق ويقال أن عرق جمع عرق وعروق لكثره عرق وعرق صب من الطين كما يقال أن العراق جمع عرق والعرق صب من الطين كما يقال أن العراق جمع العرق والعروق لكثره الانهار والتشعبات فيها العراق المعاصر تقع على نهر دجله والعرات من التخ جنوباً إلى جبال التوروس شمالاً يحتل كل ما من بلاد النهرين والتي تقد منها إلى الحضارات البشريه قدرها

ISAIAH. 19:25.   .٢٥:١٩ علما (اش)

The Lord Almighty will Bless them Saying be Egypt my People. ASSYRIA MY HAND WORK
And Israel My inheritance.   Amen.

‏اشعیا ۱۹ باب ۲۵ آیت۔ مبارک ہو مصر میری قوم اور اسور میرے ہاتھ کا کام اور اسرائیل میری میراث۔ آمین۔

·J·E·B·

705 BCE
٧٠٥ ق.م

New Assyrian Kingdom

Kushite Empire

Lydian Kingdom

Elam
علام

Medes
مادی

Van
(AS)

الامبراطورية الآشورية

Assyrian Empire

Arabs
عرب

Phrygia

Caria

Lycia

Lydia

Byblos
Sidon
Tyre

Judah
(AS)

Egypt
XXV
مصر

J.E.B

دراسات في تاريخ العالم

Army Size

Gulf War 1990-199

1990

China	3,554,
Soviet Union	3,354,130
United States	2,173,743
Iraq عراق	1,271,793
India	1,263,229
North Korea	1,190,986
Vietnam	1,057,707
Turkey	773,899
South Korea	661,467
France	554,820
Pakistan	551,720
Italy	492,477
Germany	530,826
Egypt	447,707

((End the World)) نهاية العالم
- SINgns -
* Up her the Booke

علامات الساعة   نص الزمان   70

Scentist Terrifying New Discovery in the Euphrates River
Shocled the to
Cosmos Lab. 2k View. published on Nov. 1-2022
* But WHY ARE ATY ALL So Conceered right now?
* What EXATLY is The Reson Behing it?
* Revelation : 16:12 parallel Verses
* Revelation: 16:12 NIV The Sixth angel poured out his bowL on
the great river Ephrates & its Water Was dried Up to prepare
the Way the king from the East
* Interestingly the phrase "the great river" is Never Used for
NiLe. It is Used five Time for the Euphrates Gen: 15:18
Deuteronomy 1:17 Joshua. 1:14. Revelation. 9:14, 16:12
* Revelation: 9:14 *
* Revelation: 9:14 NN It Said to Sixth Angel Who had the
Erupet, Release the four Angels Who are bound at the
Great River Euphrates *
* The Alter of Burnt Offreing Ex. 38:1-7.
* EXO. 27:2. You shall make its horns on its four
Corners; Its Horns Shall be of one piece With It. And
you shall oyrelay it With bronze.
* We know that these are demonic because the Are
described as bound Demons are fallen Angels, many
of Whom are bound chains of gloomy darkness.
2 peter : 9:4

نهاية العالم
* Committed presumably, not far from garden of Eden,
in the Euphrates regin Genesis 4:8
* EZEIEL : 47:- The RIVER OF LIEF
* Then he brught me back to the door of the temple and
there Was Water flowing from Under the threshold of Temple
Daniael: 9:27, The bible Says at the end of these Seven years human
ovrnment Will end and Jesase Will return. 11:17 PM. F.i. oV. 4-2022

(72)

من الدينه الثقافه

هل تعلم من الثقافه الثقافيه والدينيه

١- هل تعلم أن يعقوب متزوج من أختين.

٢- هل تعلم أن أجمل أمرأة خلقها الرب هي زوجة أبراهيم ساره (سراي)
(سراي (ساره) هي أخت أبراهيم من أب وليست من الأم

٢- هل تعلم النبي يونس ولد مرتين الأولى من بطن أمه
والثانيه من فم الحوت هو (يونان) النبي

٤- هل تعلم من هي جملة العرب هي أم أناس الشيبانيه.

٥- أغلى مدينه في العالم هي مدينه برمودى؟ في هذا القرن ((2022))

٦- أطيب شعب في العالم شعب مسمار على رأس قائمة أكرم وأطيب شعوب
في العالم مع شعب الوادي؟ أطيب شعب من ناحيه كرم كم أيضاً"

٧- الدوله لا يوجد فيها الفقر في هذا القرن ((2022)) هي موناكو

٨- أغنى دوله في وطن العربي هي القطر

٩- ما هي الدوله العربيه التي تسمح للمرأة في تعدد الأزواج ((زوج))
في وقت واحد : هو دوله التونس ويحرم لزوج تعدد النساء.

١٠- أنظف مدينه في العالم هي مدينه كالغارى وأيضاً" تشاقو

١١- أجمل مدينه في عالم من ناحيت موقرها في المياه هي البندقته أيطاليه

١٢- أشهر دوله العربيه والعالم هي العراق من ناحيت حضارتها العريقه.

١٢- أشرش شعوب العربيه ثقافه هي قطر والعراق.

١٤- أجمل مدينه في أفريقيا هي مدينه أديس بابا.

كما ذكرت في كتابه المقدس عهد القديم أن مخلص السينا ورسول المسيح والكلام (مسح) فقط يختلق عن السامي الأنبياء كما أذكر في عهد الجديد أي مذكور في الكتب السماوية كالتوراة والإنجيل والقرآن أن مخلص قد ولده من الزرع القدس وسوف سيكون أبنه الله ؛ بعكس السامي الأنبياء قد ولدوا من ذرية آدم وحواء (أي يكون من غيرتهم النوع والخ) وأنا السينا مخلص لا يملك غيره النوع والخ والخ كالنا في الأنبياء (بني موسى وسائر بعض الأنبياء وبني محمد)

أنا من دوري ليس لى أي أودين وليس أحمى في العربية الشامية دانيال أي الله القصاص القاص ((Daneal)) ولا أن بسبب ديني هو

مسيحي وأنا كيما أنتم تعرفون الحقيقة المدونه في العهد القديم التوراة والإنجيل والقرآن أسس أني بدوري أحترم كل ديان بأن لى أني لست قاص كى أدين بني بشر وأنا أحمل معي فكر الفيلسوف اليوناني ديمقراطيوس كما وأم أفكار من حرية الدين والصحافة وإبقاله لذلك إذا كان دماغي لا يبتزل أو يقتبس أي شيئ إلى أني منغمس في أفكار متجمدة ؛ وحين قرأه أفكار الديمقراطيه رأيت الطريق السليم إلى أن لا أنخلاط مع المجتمع الشعوب من أفكارهم الدنسه والسفله وأنا بدوري أبى لست ضد أي خص دين أو ساس و أي نوع من أفكار السلطه صرى أخواني وخواتي بني البشر صيرفوني أني لست دانيال أي لست قاص القصاء؛ وأحمل أفكار محبة الله ومخلص المسيح والكلام وتعايش مع مجتمعاتي البشر بكل أطيافه وأصنافه أني أحب كل بني البشر لى أنهم بشر مثلي أنا وهم مثابه وجه خالقنا بهذه الحاله التشابه سيكون أخو أنا وخواتنا أي من أخواتي وخواني وكلنا أولاد دخلاء وهو أبونا و الأرض أمنا لدينا كلنا ما اقتناها هي الأرض والأرض ملكي الرب صدقوني في لهوتي وأعتلى هي تأتي من الرب ولست من جدى أمي

وأقول حقا أن المسيح والله هم راضين من الأعمال وأقوال والأفعال الديمقراطيوس هي إلى الأشياء التي ترضى الله والمسيح وأنا بدوري كما قلت سابقا وأكرره مرة أخرى أنا (جوزيف أشهد بني يلك) لست ضد أي مخلوق بني بشر من سلطتهم ودينهم وعقيدتهم لى أش لكانت الرب الذي له منصب صميم وبدين في الجميع ؛ الإله هو الرب أمين كلكم أخواني وأخواتي بني البشر أحبكم والسلام الرب وسيدنا المسيح وسائر الأنبياء والملائكه معكم جميعا آمين.

جوزيف أينو يجرى يلك كانون الأول ٥ سنة ٢٠٢٢
J.E.B
أحبكم جميعكم لأنكم بني البشر آمين

ظهور الأديان الإبراهيمية السماوية الثلاثة، اليهودية والمسيحية والإسلامية
حين قال رب إلى أبراهم حين كان عمره (٧٠ ـ ٧٥) اخذ زوجتك (أي سارة)
أي (أسارة) زوجته كانت أخته من الأب وليست من الأم
وأترك أرضك وعشيرتك وبيت أبيك وأذهب الى الأرض الى أراك
(تكوين: ١٢: ١ ـ ٦) Gen.12:1-6

١ ـ الدين اليهودي لموسى ظهر في حوالي القرن السابع فبل حوالي
3,500 B.C قبل الميلاد من العصر البرونزي بني موسى. عيد هانوكا سعيد
٢ ـ الدين المسيحي للناس كما كان للناصرة نصراني حوالي ظهر
الأخر Sun. Dec. 25-2022 سنة من هذا التاريخ المدون كانون الأول
صادق عيد الميلاد في يوم الأحد المصادف يوم كانون الأول يوم ٢٥-٢٢-٢٠
عيد ميلاد سعيد ملئ من المحبة والسلام والغفران وكل عام وأنتم بخير
٣ ـ الدين الإسلامي : بدأت المكة المكرمة مان ٦١٠ بعد الميلاد دموسى
الدين الإسلامي بني محمد الذي أمر بهدم الأصنام وأشوهم
بعبادة الله على جلالة أمين
٤ ـ ثم ظهرت عدده عدده عقائد والمذاهب والأفكار واللغات دينه
والروحية والروحانيه حسب في اعتقاد بني آدم أمين ع.م.
صدق الله لعظمته وقدرته الفائقه
وقوته وجبروته أمين.

الله هو المالك
والمولى العليل ولا
أحد من بني البشر أن يكونوا المالكين أمين كما نسمي في كلمة أنكليزى LORD
كي يدعون الأنكليزين بالطبقه السابعة أو ذوو كثيره انتم تعرفون يطلقون
على أنهم كلمة لورداو الورديه flord بالمالكين صدقوني لا أحد رأيت
في حياتي عندمونم بأخذون الأشياء بكونها لا نفع الى المالك الرب والأرض
هي بالصدوق الحودي لبني مها وصدوق احوهات ملها (الرب الخالق كل شي
علي والأرض كل شي الرب حلقه مها والأرض هد) (الأم التي كل شي طهر
وخلق الرب منها الأرض كلها وحالقها المالك والسماوي والأرض أمين
فقط الرب ومخاصل المسيح هم المالكين كل هذه الأشياء لأنهم من المج وسي من
الدم وحواء لذلك الرب ومخلصا يحلون نفس المج الصفات الاهيه ولسو من
آدم وحواء اكبر واكبر لأنه آدم وحواء قد بطبعوم الله كما قال لهم وأنا الأم
يعلوا الأم خالقنا كما قال لهم وأنا من عكس سعوا وعلوا فوق الملائكه فقط كما فلو
كان فعلا وأعاله فقط لا نفع بها وأنا أعمال غير جيدة تأتي من الملك لا فقط

تكمله يعاني الحب على الصابئ وليس الحب الشيطاني

يؤمنا المحمدان في عتقادهم كان صابئ في أعتقادهم كما يدونه في كتاب
كنزربا (الدرشا) جاء في طعه المندائيه ١٣٤ يقول صابئ أنا في أنا
مختار الصيادين أنا الرئيس من جميع الصفاف أنا أعرف مياه النهار (كما يدعون)
وميره تنفيقات ومن أعتقادهم أن يوحنا عاشه في قصبات الحوار
الحسن في المراه المندائيه أقدم من يوحنا وجوها أن يوحنا معمدان أو
قبل المرشد عند المندائيين والمعمد أن ديانه المندائيه ترجع لقيادة
سام وادريس (أخنوخ) ويوحنا كل هذه أنبياء العالي كما
يقولون الحي العظيم ديانه المندائيه كانت ديانه أدم يسش
والهيبل والبرشا وطعامهم هو طعام القراني وحنوق
وعندهم صوم الصفن والهوجه أيام في شهر

(٣) عيد البوبا عيد الخليقه يصومون جمله أيام
الثالث
يعدها يأتي عيد الخليقه وأما الصوم الكبير هو يتباعد عن الخطايا
أي تنظيف البدن والوجه واليدين والأرجل يمر ثلاثة أوقات في أما الموضوع
يسيم الحمر أو التطيب في مساء ما يكتابهم هو كتاب المقدس
كنزربا
المندائيين يكون في الروح الطيبه
(درش)

* غصن على
شكل صليب
معنا الله موجود
في أتجاه ٤
يوجد في
عراق ١٥ الى
١٥ الف
مندائيين

الكنز العظيم
الكتاب المقدس الصابئ للطائفه المندائيين
شريعتهم حيث قدموا النصارى
منهم أنوخ أخناوخ أيام أبو نعاق
ابن أحرق أنصاري وصاحب الكتاب الأكياب والاعيان
ومن
من الأمن بعض أغصان رمز الديانه القطعى من الجريد (درش)

قطعه من ذهب
على شكل
الشكل
حبال من حرير

قطعه
قماش
حرير

2:24 pm   عـطـل
Dec 23 – 2022

الـحـر الـفـنـي

معنى الصابئة هي الصبغة أو تعميد الصابئة المندائيه
ى الملك الكبرى كي تنطق ربهم بجم الـ؟؟؟ الـ؟؟ كم
الشـطـان ؟

□ * ٩ * ٤ *
△ * ؟ * ؟ *
J̄ * E · B *

الـحـر القرباني الصابئي، الحر الصابئي هو الأضحيه سى التبادل الروحي
قوه أحد أنواع الصابئة القديم . وتعتمد الـ؟ القربان على الصحه
لمده القرابين بالأوقات مختلفة . طقوس وتعزيمات معينه وهو من أقوى
أنواع الـ؟ السفلى مكتب به قوه أقوى أنواع الدروع والأقوى والجن
السفلى منهل الحياة لمن ؟ يتقدم اليوم الفقيه جدأ أو المـتـصصه
وسـتـقـدم للملك ورد المطلقه والحاكم والرحول على الـلـطيق والجـبة
الرهبيه والورق الدرق الـسطره على بأى الدروع . وأقوى أختدام
له هوه الوقايه من الشر قريب أو
المرض المزيد

١- معنى كلمه نوحى بصره كلمه المندائيه يعني نوحى هي نوحى (حامص)
بصره معنى بصره أن فى كلمه الأرميه هى كم
٢- أما أكلت مه الشـمرين هى الهريسه كما قيل عندما رح سفينة نوح
أضعوا ماديه الغفران هى طبخ سبعه أنواع من الحبوب تقر با من الله
عرفه هذه العومه بارين وكريمه من أشه ما كلات التى تطبخ مى
جنوب العراق وهذا المشترك بين المسلمين والصابئة وأيضأ يوحد
فى جنوب العراق التى تطبخ مها هى ثـلـه التى تطبخ الحمص
ولبيع مع البعض فى جرد واحد
ودياناتهم هو ولادناته فى العراق هو متدائين لأنه بأمنون
أول آدم ولادنه كانت فى العراق الحميب سوا با أشارك
فكم بأن أول آدم كان ولادنه مع الحواء فى العراف التى كانت جله
مى ذلك الوقت (ج . ٤ . ب)
٣- الأدريـس بسمونه دانانوح (أنوح أو أنوح) الذي
(ذهب مع الله)
٤- ويتجددون خمسه معلمين آدم، شتش، ينوح، بسام، وأنوح ويوحنا
٥- تكلمه الربي كلمه المندائيه معنا المقدس يختلف مى معنى عربيه ربي

كل أفراد وطقوس وعادات الصابئة المندائيين
رئيس الطائفة الشيخ ثم كما أن رئيس الطائفة في بلاده يجب أن
يأخذ الناس (الناس) كالرئيس الدين هو الناس في طقوس الدينية
نهم في الماء أي ينقضي في الماء ((الناس من النباتات الجبلة)) وصبا
على جسمه على طقه الدين لكي ينمو من هذه النباتات ومن بعد رايته
دكله طيبه ودام الخضراء وبعد أن تنتهي الرحى يجب أن تتوم الرائحة تني بوصا
((الزيت درفش)) تسميه استعيد يقال صبغه أو صبغه لله
وكله المندائيين في الأرضه بعني الموحدين
مرحله النازلية نزول الماء التمد أو صبغه لله أو القمر
المرحله الوسطى
المرحله الاخيره نصعد إلى الفوق ونقرأ القرآء ويعطيهم الخبز المبارك
يوكما في مرائي من الأخر أمد صباه تكون هنالك نوع تبادل روحي
هو يعطيني كوشتا وأنا أرد له دوكا ومن هناك سوفا نترك
منانبه في مضاء أبو عريب لزعاج وعمرا فرقه موسيقيه وفكرولين ونطفه
تمني هنالك ثميا وأيضا عندما تبدأ الرقص يكون رئيس الرقص
أو يعود الرقص روحاني والمطرب والطوبعتباه

صفة تكمله أسرار وطقوس وعادات الصابئه المندائيون

ساعة من شروق الشمس ومن بعد ساعات وقبل غروب الشمس
في ساعة

أما في الأعياد فقط ننصب هذا درفش هو من الدين هو عباره من
قطعه من القماش. ومن هناك من أن يريد أن يحلف اليمين
على درفش والدرفش هو عباره على علم النبي يحيى يوحنا
الرومز على الطائفه. المندائين ومن رسائل يوحنا كان يحلف في يد
من القطن وعلى نحت القماش يحلف على 64 حاجب يصفون عليها من
آيات وصور. يارت هي ست يسمى الطقوس التعميد ويحافظ عليها يقطع عهد
إلى الرب خالق وأيضا يوجد التعميد يوم الأحد وأيضا شهر من جف
أو قطو رأس من القه شه ويقلعوا في الجبال كل من الحق الذي
يصعونه على الملس. مسبوق على الجبال في هذا المكان أرض مبارك
والماء الجاري يجري الطقوس السنه. وسوف سمول ساعه وتعمد
للمندائين ليوم الرابع وعندنا كما قلت إلى الموتى يوجد الطعام لقربان
في هذا المكان يجري ساعه أو التعميد إلى المتروحين نساء والرجال
وفي مناسبات الدينيه هو عكس طقوس دينيه. ولايجوز في الماء الراكد
ولقأئل لكان التعميد في كل أعياد وأيضا صلات في كل يوم صبح وظهر
وعصر. ويوجد هناك على ضفاف النهر ذبيحه من أجل طعام عقرن
يجب أن نقول بأتم الحي. ويجب أن يجري الرومز الذبيحه يجب أن لايكون
أي نقص في الذبيحه الملابس نلبسها أحنا المندائي يسمى
الرستا يتكون من جمه قطو أو ملاس أما الباس الشيخ تختلف
يتكون من نفس الملابس فقط تضاف عليها شملتي أو أشني أشراء
فقط نفس شملتي بندمه تكون أطول كي يغطي فيه وأنفه في خلاك
تعميدو وتابيع خاصه والشيع من الملك من الأرض. وجزء ثاني
الذي يتمين الشى تاحه. وهي تابع من الرب يحلق ويضع على راسه كما قال
النور انيه يضع كمامه في رأس هذه النور انيه. وهذا التاج هو
ومن اكثر الشيخ المركبه ومحبتي أم سوم ياوى ياور يهي أ م
الحي والمركبه معناها العصى هذه العصا هي من غصن الزيتون
الشيخ يختار رئيس الطائفه الصابئه وهي عالم وفي العراق

Mandean ((Sabean))

الصابئة (الصبه) (المندائين) (الصفه)

اسرار طقوس وعادات وديانة الصابئة المندائية

نبدأ في العيد عند الصابئة السحاء أو البرونيا يا عبد برايه

عبد الخليفة لله سكان وتقال حضور الغوجمه أيام معينه

يجري ب كافه من المشي الدرسه بتوصل بالليل والنهار و في معبد

الليل النهار تقدر ان يبدع في الليل والنهار تستمر الى حمسه أيام

طقوس في هذه الأيام هو تمهيد بطقوس تجري في المعبد

في يا به اهل من نوع المتعرض الماء باري في حضور الشيخ

ويوجد شيء من العبد الاول وضع اكليل النرجس (باس)

يليه وضع الاكل من السد الى جساء وباتي ويكمل بامي البر

هنا ويوجد هنا طعام العزن من معين من صح حدود معينه

طعام القزن يكون من كل الخضروات والفاكهه والبكاء ممكن

صعوب من اللحوم . وذبائح يكون أنصار بكون اكثر مقدس

كل حفلات وطقوس تهلوما في هذا المكان في بغداد وهناك

على صفاف النهر يوجد شيخ الدين يتخص لطقوس الصلات

ويمارس قبل التعميد لعوائل الذين يراد تعميدهم من تجمعهم على

صفاف النهر كما قال واحد من شيخ الصابئة لا أحد ان يقدر أن يدخل

الموتى بعد ان يدخل أي أنسان الى هنا اذا اخر أن والى المنس والى

حتى اذا كان من نفس الطائفه لا يقدر ان يدخل اذا كان ليس متقدرا

متقدراً. وقال أيضا يجب أن تعمد قبل الوصوء (النوظي وعدر

منطق الصلات ب كل شي أو أشياء هي متعمد كالقوري والواتي

والحبوب والخبز وحتى طيبه في الطين حين يذهب الى الشريقه

تبدأ الشريقه في التر الاكل ثم يقرأ الصقوس والبات ومن ثم

باخدون بسم من جبر والحضر وان وملك والفاكه من كل نوع

اللعبه صفنه ثم تضع في القم عند أنشاء الصلاة في فم اول القبله

تبدس كل مجموع كل اعشيه في المائده ومن بعدها أن يعد لطيف

بالبه للأيام السحه يمارسون طقوسهم تركز على الناس المتوفين (الموتى)

من ظلام الى عالم النور الجنه ويوجد ثلاثة صلات في اليوم نحله

ستار جبار الحلو - رئيس طائفة الصابئة المندائيين

Sabean

الصابئة المندائيون

Mandae

Dec. 2022.

من كردستان شمال العراق وصارت المؤسسات وأتباع هذه
الديانه الزرادشتيه ويعترف مهنا في العراق وصار منصب
وممثل الزرادشتيه في حكومه العراق الحبس (يعيش عرق الى
أبر بلاد الحضارات (جوزيف أشو حي بك) في كردستان وصار موطن أوممثله
ووجوده الذي ويعترف بها الرصي أمر السيد عواص طيب وهي
أول أمرأة تشغل هذا المنصب في العراق الحبس عن الديانه الزرادشتيه
صار عندها مؤسسات تعني بهم وصار يقومون الاحتفالات في
كردستان والزرادشتيه يمارسون طقوسا عاديه يعلنا ويوجد
أي شكل من الأشكال تضيق بهم وصار عندهم معبد في العراق سليمانيه
صاروا في كل طقوسهم الدينيه ومن أهم المناسبات التي أحتفلوا بها
العراق كان في ٢١ أذار ٢٠١٩ كانت من الفترة قليله عندما احتفلوا
بها أعداد السويدوز على أختلاف انتمائهم وشاركوا معهم في هذا
الاحتفال على أي نوع القبائل كانوا معهم من العراق الأخرى الديني والمسلمين
البراشيين والمكوناب القوميه الأخرى هذا هو العراق السموع بما فيه
من تنوعاته الموجود بين المكونات العراق القومي من المكونات
والأعراق والشعوب المختلفه نبارك عطفه الله عليهم بارك
يعيش العراق في كله من أعراقه ومكونات القراقته والله يحفظهم
وبارك كل الناس بني أدم على الأرض في السلام باقي في
بنيهم ما في أديانهم وسكناتهم وأعرمهم وبلادهم وكل مخلوق ما في
بني أدم وحواء أمن حوزتي إنشو ابن بك المدون هذه المقاله

Time:12:09 Am
Fri. Dec 23-2022
ٮ٭ᚾ٭𝐁٭
ٮ٭ا٭س٭
⚠٭٭𝐀٭ح

الزرادشتيه (١٢) تكمله لديانه الزرادشتيه من سبعه

الزرادشتيه هي ديانه سماويه بانه يعبرون الله وكل مصادر الديانه الابراهيميه (الى اليهود) المسيحي (الاسلام) كلهم يعبرون ويامنون في وجد الخالق وابوبا السماوي لذلك كلهم كبوه في وجوده وخلقته السماء والأرض وكل شي برى ومايرون وكذلك كذلك الزرادشته يامنون في وجود الله كما وأت عنه في كتابه الذي املكه (أني جوزيف ابشو) وي بك يمرون كل هذه المعلومات والبيانات كما قرأنا و معترا ودرس ثم دونتها كما كاني عند بعض العلماء الاعلام حول مزهب أو عقيده أو أفكار الزرادشته اللهم ذين يحوى بموسى أوعبده النار كما قيل من الزرادشته ولا قدر أن اتهم مايقولونه ولكن يقولون مجوس جاء من الزرادشته ولا قدر أن اتهم مايقولونه ولكن عندها اصفظ على قلمي وأدون أفكارهم كما اوهما وأراؤها في كتبهم وأمالت هناك في ذلك وعسى عمر طويل مبل الحق سنه كي أعرف عن عرف دينهم وعقدهم وأفكارهم ولت كني كنب بعم صدقوى وانما عندما قلمي يكون جرى في تدوين الحقائق أنا أعرف كماهي مكتوبه ومدونه في عبر وقديم لكنتي حول حقيقه أي الحوس اللهي حقائق صحيحه ومدونه كما قول واسمه الكتاب المدن عبر القديم والعهد الجديد في أنكلزى (Holy Notic Book) (من ذلك كل من بدون هو حقيقي من كلام الانبياء والرسل وتلميذ السدنالمى والقديسي وكل صلى اذا كابوا في اديان الابراهيميه (يهوديه المسيحيه والاسلاميه) (أمن المجوس) كما دونته الاخبار الجيد حول ولده سيدنا المسيح عند ماقدموا المجوس الهدايا له هو الزهب والمره والبخور هم كانوا نفس المجوس الدين دكرهم في تدويني المجوس الزرادشته في العراق الزرادشته بعض الاحيان تقوى وبعض الاحيان تضعيف وكي تتفرص و تخاصمنا أخرى حسب اعتقادي ذلك اذا دوجد نفس الافكار المستمره من وأول أفكار وامالس وجودهم لم تتداول أفكارهم وعقيدتهم ودينهم فلذلك ينقرضون فقد اعلنت هذه الديانه عن نفسها في عرق نفسها أتباع والمتبقى أعترا فانها بكل ديانه لحميه زرادشته في كردستان العراق وصارت مؤسسات وأتباع

(٤)

الزرادشتية في عراق

الزرادشتية: دين قديم اكثر من ثلاثة الآف (300 years) سنة

كلمة الزرادشتى هي مشتقة (نسبة) النبي (زرادشت) هذه الديانة الى هو زرادشتى

هو واحد من الفارسي الزردشتى على هذه النسبة ولكن الزردشتى في عراق

يعرون عندنا تاريخ أول وأخر نشأة هذه الديانة عندها كتاب الآفستا او (أفستا

(AVISTA) تاريخ ظهور هذه الديانة أم مختلف أيضا بعض آراء يقول أن هذه

الديانة ظهرت 1000 قبل الميلاد (1000 B.C) وبعض أراء أخرى ظهور هذه

الديانة ما بين 1000 أو 1800 قبل الميلاد وكانت هذه الديانة كانت في كبيرين

أديان (الزمان) من الديانات القديمة من الديانات قوية جدا انتشرت

هذه الديانة وموجوده حد الآن في الهند وأيران وأذربيجان والعراق

والدول الاخرى أيضا في بعض معتنقين هذه الديانة من هذه الدول وغيرها

سافرو الى النصف السائر كندا وأمريكا والى أوربا فاصبح من هذه الديانة في وقت

الحالي في هذه الدول على العجم من الزرادشتية كانت الديانة قبل البوذية

والمسيحية والأسلامية اللذان أتباع في وقت الحاضر قلوبي قلوبي في شكل

اكثر آي أحفظوا كل كثير كثرة أحصائيات المنشوره والمرويه تقول

الى أبهم أقل من 2000 ألف الزرادشتية الزرادشتية في الديانات

لوحيدة آي هنا مقال أورشه تقول أم من عنده النار ولكن هذا الكلام

لا صحيح ليسوا عنده النار وأي يقدرون النار ويستقبلونها

في طقوس العبادية ولكن لم يعبدوا النار لانهم يعتقدون في وجود الله واحد

لشبية بين الاديان والزرادشتية تشابههم مع بعض البعض كما يعتقرون

بعض العلماء هكذا التقارب ما في بينهم الدين اليهودى والمسيحى والأسلامى

يعتقدون كل هذه الاديان جاءت من الديانة الزرادشتية كما في اعتقادى

لما وهكذا (أ+ع+م) لانة لهم صلاتهم معهم مثل الزرادشتية

عندهم خمسه صلوات (5) وعندهم فكم الحج وعندهم صيام مدة

شهر واحد والزرادشتية فكرة المهدى المنتظر لكن المهدى اسلامى

الذين يعتقدون في روح عقيدتهم سيكون صراع بين الخير والشر وينتصر

الخير على وأيها هي الفكرة قوية كما ذكر في كتاب المقدس المسيحى كتاب

يوحنا الرؤيا، كما قال الزرادشتية الديانة متقاربه من ناحية الأيمان

والمانوية الديانة زرادشتية هي كذلك يعتقدون الديانة المانوية

تكملة الزرد وشتيه من صفحة ١١٤

... طيور الجارحة ... الحياة الأبدية ... المعرفة ... عنده في كل أماكن عبادة الزرادشتية وهو نظامهم وهو المؤمن ملقاً رجل على هيئة طائر يقف على حجته التي تتحدث منها شعله دائماً الخلود ... عند الزرادشتية بالفارس النار وفيها شعله لا تنطفئ وأعل أيضاً لطقوس زرادشتيه أنهم الزرادشتية قديماً ... الجثث تسمع أصوات ... الجثث على طهر التي يملأها أشعة ... وطيور الجارحة ... من تجمع أعظامهم في حفرة ويبني في قوة خاصة ...

٥٠ عاماً من هذا اليوم ((2022)) يدفنون زرادشتيون موتاهم في ... معدنية توضع في القبر.

* الأعياد: الأعياد الدينية، أشهر أعيادهم هو عيد النور وعيد ميلاده العام الاعتدال الربيعي حيث يتم احياء مولد الزرادشتية في احتفال وقف في النار ويوجد أعياد أخرى مثل مهرجان وتحان وأدريان

* ... كي يواجه ... علية أن أنس ... ويكثرون من ... ويكثر أتباعه المتزوجين والدين لديهم الولد وذريته صالحة ... الطلاق محرماً كلياً في ديانة الزرادشتية

* اللغات الزرادشتية عندهم وهي ابن لغة داري أو بيدياء ((تعدد اللغات)) هؤلاء القاطنون في أفغان والفارسين ... هاجروا إلى هند حيث أنتشرت ... في ذلك بلاد الفارس يتكلمون الزرادشتية المعاصر ... الإله المزد ... هو الحكم والنور متن ... شوكة ... النور ...

JUIJIRO MATSUDA

* أهور مازدا ((إله النور)) ملاحظة * الأرض هي أمنا لأن جثة هي لله

* الجثث الموتى يجب ترجع إلى الأرض حيث جثته من الأرض ويرجع إلى الأرض

* ... في اعتقادهم الجثث الموتى تجنس التراب والماء ليس ذلك!

الجواب في هذه عقيدة كما هم الزرادشت يأمنون في الله واحد (هو الله) ١٠ حيث جثته الأم)) يعنون ذلك ... يعنون ذلك أن رب خلق الإنسان من الطين أي جثث حين الإنسان أصلاً من الطين ... ذكر في كتاب المقدس التوراة وذكر في الإنكليزي أصلاً في العبراني

Jabn-: Jab'neal + جسة الله في عربية

ه. ٤.٤.ه

(ك) (ل) (اث عشر)

تكملة الزرادشتية من صفحة ١٠

وجوده للنفاق والخديعة (اهريمه) ولكن بالرجل والعقل والبرهان
والدواع وأنه وهذه وهي وجودات عند الزرادشتية ويطعنون عليه (اهريمه)
حيث تصوره فلسفة لأنه الحياة على أنها صراع بين الله
والشيطان ينتهي في النهاية الحق معهم يبين الزرادشتية هي
سورة في هذا الصراع كما عظم رادشتور والفلاسفة الطبيعة الماء
والنار والأرض والهواء ونوع النار مثل (نور الله) لذلك يتم
اعتقاد آدم عبدة النار لكثرة تقديسهم (النار) كما تكون
الزرادشتية أول ديانة توحيدية أنزلت كلمة أول من اعترفوا

* وجود الملائكة (امشاسبنتا) الخالدس المقدسين المباركين
(أهور مزدا) الذي خص كل أنسان في الملك الخارس ؛ أما
أخرى هناك يحكمه الهه نتج الروح (مثرا * Mtra)
ومقارنته الأنسان من حياته وسيئاته حيث ينقص الناس
يبين الحساب (فردوس) والجحيم ؟ حيث يصل أنتماء على
طبقات هي ما بينهما، والسر الخفي في النهاية فئة
جميلة بيضاء وهي (النور أو النور) من الفارسية ؛ أما الموسى
(غير جيدس) موجد أمة قيمها تقوده إلى الجحيم ومن هذه الفلسفة
آتت تابعة بين ديانة الزرادشتية والديانات الابراهيمية حيث أن
الزرادشتية صلوات جماعة أيضا وذلك في معبد النار يتشابه مع
المسيحية يكبون يحرمون الصيام والتمثيل الأمتناع عن النوع

* رموز الزرادشتية وضع تمثل للزرادشتية لها عباد دنيا
ميزوا له للتلاحم خاصة كما تقسم الديانات وهذا الذي يتكون من
الكوشتي أو ميطلق عليه الحزام المقدس حيث يرتدى بطريقة
محددة بلف ثلاثة مرات حول الخصر هقد من الصوف في عقده زوجة
ويتكون من 72 > V < خطا أسطر صوفيا في الدلالى 72 > V< فصل
من (ياسا) وهي مجموعة يات نصوص المقدسة كتاب المقدس
عندهم (أفستا * AVISTA) القسم الثاني الذي قميص
(سدل) ويرتدى منذ بلوغ ؛ أما الهسه يرتدون لباس ليلس أبيض وعمله
أبيض ويرخون على تغطية وجوهم كي لايوقفوا النار المقدس بأنفاسهم
وكذلك الراهب الصمت من الريون الزرادشتية حيث يمنع
* طهرها كما أن نارا توجه إلى النور إليهم وتتق جثة حيث المقدسة الموتى والمقدس الكبرى

الزرادشتية أو المجوس أصلهم وطقوس وصلوا وعبادتهم يعبدون Mazda الديانة هل تقول زرادشت وربما سمعنا عنه المجوس هل سمعت الديانة الزرادشتية تكون أحدثها؟ لا؟ هل تعلم أن زرادشتية أول ديانات أول ديانات؟ ربما هل سمعت ماذا من كل ما يا؟ هل تعلم أن زرادشتية أول ديانات مصطلح المجوسية وما سمعت هذه الديانة الطقطقة فكرة التوحيدية؟ من حقائق كانت هذه الديانة الطقطقة فكرة العقاب والثواب والدنيا والآخرة وجنة والنار من يريد زرادشتية وما يسمع وأين وأطهر الزرادشتيون هم معتنقون في الديانة وهي من الديانات ثابتة في بلد الفارس مثل ٤:٤ الدين وهي ديانة التوحيدية القديمة وأطلقه عليها زرادشتيون وليو من عنده النار كما يقال أو شاء عنه وأطلق العرب اسم المجوس التي غير معنا الأصلي من الكلمة مشتقة من كلمة (مجوس) الفارسية

مجوس نعم الزرادشتيون الأحلام والرؤى وعدد وبعد منهم يقارب ٢٠٠ 200 ألف ويتركزون في إيران وموطنهم الأصلي والسند إلى لالا بعد أن ديانتهم ووصول الفتح الأئمة إلى بلد الفارس؟ وسميت هذه الديانة إلى الزرادشتية من هوبرج تعظيم زرادشت القديمة أنه ناقله من هنا بفضل نقيد إلا الله حيث أنه ناقله القائد الديانة القديمة وآمنوا في وجود إله واحد (وهو الله) وأحد ولكن في وجهة نظر الأخرى الديانة الزرادشتية أنه أطلقه عليها اسم حكيم والموحدون (أهورا مازدا) Mazda سيرت إله حكيم والموحدون زرادشت هذه الديانة على أخلاق واعتني على أكثر وجعل لذلك دوراً في آخرتهم حيث إن أن يحاسب على قوله وعمله صالح

أثبتت زرادشت 706 و ٧.٦ V.٦ باقية حتى الدين تعظيم من العقل الربانيات شكوك والغضب وكل ما يريد نفس الإنسانية من السوء وذلك من على الهدى والصدق بالنور ضوء حيث أخضعت وأثبتت تعاليم الزرادشتية في ثلاثة أساسية في فكرتهم؟ الفكرة القول أعن ديانتهم والتزمتهم معنى الكتاب المقدس (AVESTA) فيها وعامة الأصل وهو مطوراً أول يعلمهم عنده فيصوم تعاليم الزرادشتية والتزمتهم الصلوات أول إله (هورا مزداي أمزدا) والذي يعطيه الخالق الكون والعقل العقل والفعل والصدق طيب ٣-٤. حق ٤. وتقوى والحي ٧- والخلود أما الشيطان وهو أثر المطلق ويجد به الشقاء ٧ إله؟؟ ٧ صفات هي ١-النور ٢-

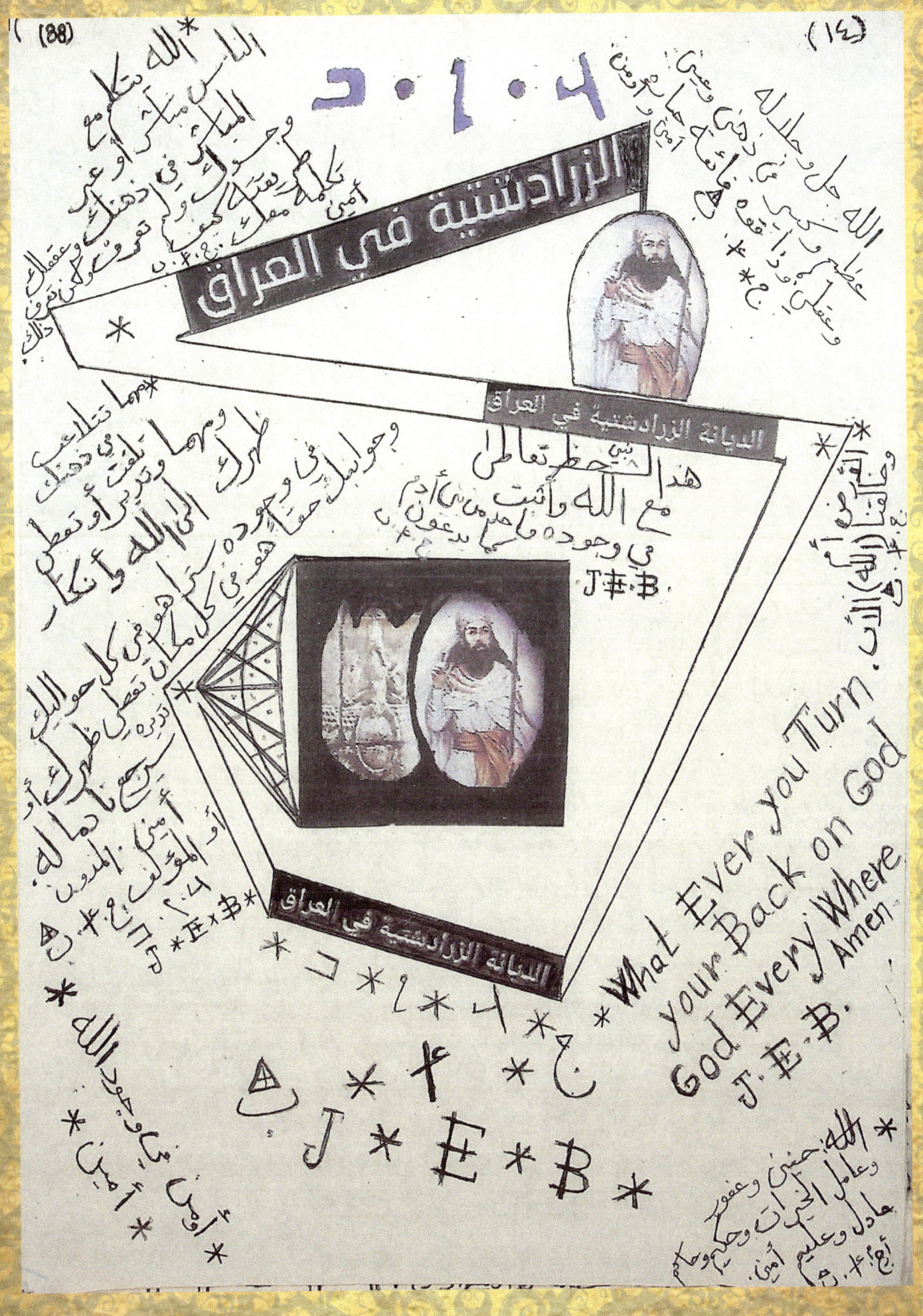

بسم الله الرحمن الرحيم

كلمة اليهودي من صنع اليهود... كل أشكال الصارة وعلوم التكنولوجيا وبدعة
تفسير طبقة اليهود وكريم... الفن وموسيقى بعض أدبيات و... علم الشطابه
وكريم المدارس خاصه ... بأشياء لتعلم دين تقليدي وشريعه
وهم يفضلون ... اليهود يتعلمون ... أبناء طائفة اليهود العلوم الدنيوبه
عند الحاجه فقط من أجل أنقاص المكاسب من أجل كسب الرزق
وعند اليهود السبت تتوقف عند ... أصفر، عند وصول ... عدد
المرأة ... على الطاقه ... وجودين في روسيا وجمهوريات اتحاد
جمهوريات السوفيتي ... وصلوا في مدنهم الخاصه ... بعض التعليم
التورة هو الصح ونقاب النساء ... أكثر من نقاب المسلمات
وفي داخل اليهود ... يتكلمون باللسان وغريب ... أن يتعاملوا
في اللغه العربيه ويعسرون ما لقه ... لهم ... يستعملون اللغه السائده
... لغه يادشه وهي جسم موضوع ... هي لغه يهود أوربا خليط
القرون (2) من اللغه ... (10) و(11) الميلادي وهي لغه غلط
من أرامية وأطالة والساسه والفرنسيه واليهوديه يتكلمون بتلك... لاين
كثير في المال وأعلم من اليهود الأشكناز، وإسرائيل ليس لها دور
... هو محرم، وآخرون اليهود لهم دمقراطيه، والمرأة
عندهم دور يعمله من الحمله ... على اختلاف الطوائف الأخرى
... عمليات التي يحبون (2) ... في الجنس نفس عند
الرجال اليهود موصوفه، وكثير من نساء اليهود لا يردون التعلم عند
الحاخامات لليهود الرجال ولكن يوجد مدارس خاصه لهنه (لهم) وهم
يظهر كثير من التشدد عن المرأة، والنساء في أوتوبيسات سيارات عامه ويمنع أخذ
كندس بين رجال، والنساء في نيويورك يوجد كبير لطف يقولون
الصور إلى النساء، ويوجد المحريدم اليهوديه القديميه موجوده في
مدينه حارة القدس وشقارم ومدينه بن براك معاويه في مدينه تل أبيب وبعدها
مدينه نيويورك New yours وعارم برفضون الدوله العلمانيه
ويقولون أنهم يأسفون في تعلم اليهودي أن دوله يهوديه أن تتم أقامتها على
يد إبراهيم المخلص، المحريديم واليمني

احتفظ

تكمله لحريديم من صفحه ( ) الحمريديم الحريدى

تفضل طائفه الحريديم كل أشكال الحضاره وعلوم التكنلوجيا بزعمه
وكذلك الفن والموسيقى بعض الدراسات والفلسفه علوم الشطابنه
وهم بفضلوا المدارس خاصه بهم بالثبات بتعلم دين تقليدى وشريعته
ويلجؤون لما عند الحريديم بتعلم أبناء طائفه الحريديه العلوم الدنيويه
عند الحاجه فقط من أجل أنقاص كان كاتب من أجل كسب الرزق
وعند الحريديم السبت بتوح عند اللبن صفر ، عند وصول سن عدد
المرأه في سنه يبسرورها عامر ، ولا يتزوجون مع الآخرين إلا
مريم الحريديم ، وأعلب الطائفة سوجودين في روسيا وجمهوريات أتحاد
الجمهوريات السوفيتى ويصلون من مناطقهم الخاصه ، بعتبر التقيم
التورك هو الصح ، ونقاب النساء الحريدى أكبر من نقاب المسلمات
وفي داخل الحريديم أرائيلية بتهتم بالطبان التلبس بثياب ابن تكلمون
في اللغه العربيه ويعتبرونها لغه مقدسه لم يستعملون اللغه الدارشه
بكانوا لغه يادشه وهى حسب موضوع يداهى لغه يهود أوربا خلال
القرنين (2) من القرن (10) و(11) الميلادى وهى لغه غلط
من أرامية وأنجاله والماسه والفرنشه واليهوديه بتكلم بها تكلمين
كثير من العالم وأعلم من اليهود الاشكناز ، فوامرأه لايلبسن لا دور
من الحياه هو محرم وأحان الحريديم لبس لها دستقراطيه ، والمرأه
عندهم دور بعضه من الحياه العامى بها على أختلاف الطوائف الأخرى
من أرائيليات الى بيسور ((2)) شنه في الجيش نفس عند
الرجال الحريديم موضه ، وكتير من نساء الحريديم لايردون التقلم عند
الحاجليات لهم رجال ، لكن يوجد مدارس خاصه لهبنة لهم (لهم) وقد
يطهر كثير من تشدد عن المرأه وفي نيويرك يوجد كبير لطس بقالوا
كثيرين من رجال والنساء في أوتوبيسات سيارات عامه وبنع أخذ
الصهم الى النساء ، ويوجد الحريديم اليهوديه الحرسيميه موجوده في
بينه حاره القدس وشعارم ومدينه بنى براك ومعاوره في مدينه تل أسيب ويعرحاره
مدينه نيويرك New yours وشعارم برفضوا الدوله العبرانيه
وبقولين أنهم بأمنون في تقلم اليهودى أن دوله يهوديه أن تقم أقامترا على
يديرالسيم المخلص ، المريديم لسوا الملى

(٤)
الحريديم : الحريدى : المتشرد

طائفة يهودية واحدة يتحرم أخطلاط الرجال والنساء وينحم
على المرأة والعلم والتعليم وكشف وجه المرأة وبعد بلوغ البنت عمرها
أو طفله سبعة (7) years سنوات ولا تقدر أن تخرج من البيت الذى هم
وتعطى جمرها أكثر طائفة اليهودية متشدده وأكثر تشددا من
الأديان الأخرى يهود الحريديم كثير تشابه مع المجتمع الاسلامى
الحريديم يخافون من الله . ومعنى الحريديم هى معنى جمع الحريدى أنها المتقى
وربما مشتق من كلمة الحريله الموجوده فى اللغة العربيه معنى أعتزله أو اكتفى
هم من اليهود الأورثوذكس المتدينين يتقدم أو يلتزمون بشكل صارم وكرسوا
فى حياتهم فى دراسة التلمود وهم أكثر التزاما فى الشريعة اليهودية أنهم
يلبسون معاطف طويله سوداء وقبعات تعني اللون سوداء وامرأة
أمر النساء يلبسون النقاب السوداء بكل المرأة أو النساء فى تغطيه
كل جسدها من الأطراف وساقة ووجها وكل أعضاء من جسدها فى غباء
ونقاب سوداء . ومعظم الحاخامات اليهودية ينتمون إلى طائفة
الحريديم إلى طائفة ١٠% من المجتمع الاسرائيلى حوالى مليون
بعض الطائفة أكثر نمواً طائفة أسرائيل وأعلم من التكبار
وليبنيه يستعملون أكثر حروف فى كتابه والحريدايم أكثر نمواً فى
الولاده من ثلاثه مرات عن الباقى طوائف اليهوديه ، عند الحريديم يطهرون
الولد حتى 30 يوماً ولو كانت المولود الأنثى تمتد إلى 90 يوماً بحب
أمر أن تتمع زوجها ولا يحب أو يكفرو فى اليهود العلمانى ولم
يتزوجون الحريديم الأسم ((الحريديم)) والحريديم يعشون مع البعض ومنفزلين
على باقى الطوائف اليهود . ولا أحد أن تقدر يأخذ أو تصور امرأة ويصلوا
المدارس خاص من مدارس اليهوديه بسم أم كنيسات لتعليم الدين التقليدى
الدين اليهودى . ويعتبرون الفلسفه هى الشيطانيه وأخفاء كل جسدها وخطامات
معصومين الحريديم أصدرو فتوى لباس العباد والنقاب إلى أعطو كل أجزاء أبر
أصفنا للعدم أحمد والجمل من كائنات عامه لديه يعسرو المرأة عوره مثل كل
جسدها كله عوره وحبب فى الحريديم حفاظ الفتوى أحترم المرأة لجمرها
لحسدها وداترا تنفيذاً لتعاليم الدين اليهودى الذى يدعوا فى
أحتشام والأخلاق وكثير من حاخامات يصعون ملصقات فى شوارع
وعلى جدران لترويد أفكارهم ومعتقداتهم . تكمله فى صفحه ١١-- شكرأ

الحريم

يهوديات يعبدن الرجال و يغسلن أقدامهن

الحريم في العبريه
العبدى: معنى من العربيه :: النقى
أو المشرد * أج * ٭ ⴲ ⴲ ٭
٭ ⴲ ⴲ ٭ ⴲ ٭ ⴲⴲⴲ ٭
ⴲ *أ* ٭ ⴲ ٭ ⴲ ٭ ⴲ ٭ ح ٭
٭J ٭⊞٭B ٭ J ٭⊞٭B٭

((الأزيديه)) اليزيديه

تكمله الأزيديه :-

وتترزن على المعبد زقوره بنيت في طرف مهاري يطرح ٢٢ أثا وعشرين ضلعا ترمز إلى إله الشمس وإلى الأزيديه معها روحاني يتألف من ستة التخاص هم أصحاب القرب باسم أميس طائفه اليزيديه التي تطلق علي نفسها المخلص على أولياء كما يقولون هي أتربا مهاري في الأعياد وعبادتهم لكي ينفون أنهم ذلك الأزيديه يعبدون الله الذي تسميه الخودي (أي الله) لكن في ديانته الإسلاميه تسمى الله كما يسيرون ويقولون اشركه له يعترون هي قوه واحده هو الله واحد

يفتخرون الأزيديين في أن الإمام أصلي في نظراته من بين البشر أهل الفضل يعود إلى مريم الروح من معتقدات والأديان الأخرى والأزيدين ٨ أعياد دسنه تبطت في طوطها طبيعه الصوم معروض على الأزيدن في ثلاثه أيام في منتصف شهر كانون الثاني (Jan) فيفرض على رجال الدين ٤٠ يوما في الصيف ومثلها في الشتاء وتؤدي كل ترانيل عبادات في اللغه الكرديه ويتم الزرع في نيسان وأيضا يتم الصيد وحراثه الأرض وزراعتها

لله عيد يأتي في الشتاء وحاشيته يرحلون للمسجد إلى أداء مراسم لله عند حيث يقوم الحاضرين مع ترانيل الدرسه يقدرون رجال الدين في أشعال ٣٦٥ قنديل في هذا المكان لمده دياما لله موجود في نور (۳)

يأمنون الأزيدين بأن مصدر الخير والشر والحياه والموت والأخره ومنهم يعتقدون اعتقادا راسخا بتناسق الأرواح من هذه العناصر الأربعه تكون أربعه هي الولاده والكبر والموت ويرجعوا مرات أخرى، الأربعاء يوم مقدس عند اليزيدين (Thu) الذين تعتمد التقويم الشرقي الذي يتأخر ثلاثه عشر ((۱۳)) يوما عن التقويم الميلادي

* ملاحظه : عندما آدم وحواء أكلوا من الفاكهه الجنه أصبح يعرفون !
(المعرفه) ويعرفون من الشر والخير وحين معرفتهم من الشر والخير فقد أصبحوا في عقيدتهم وعقائدهم يعبدون الا تنين لأن الاتنين يكون القوه والقوى جاء من البشر لذلك عبادتهم لأن القوه الثانية أقوى منهم مثل الدين

(تابع)

نكمله اليزيدية من صفحة ٦

عتبة المعبد المقدس يحص من قدسية خاصة ولا أن يجوز أن يمص أن تطأه أقدام أناس ممكن أن يستزله من ناحية المعبد تقع عساك مجموعة من القبور والتوابيت ومها تمثة سوداء دل عليه (بخاه داود) وبما برهان ماليس بدين خلدة أما هو في علم المعبد شموع رتبت حول ماء جاريه تكون الديانة اليزيدية التي تجمع عناصر النبات والنار والماء والهواء وتنبط مكان سبعة أعمده من الحجر غطيت من أقمشه ملونه ترمز الى الملائكة التي سبعة في مجلس المحدى (الله كما يقولون) وكل من يدخل المعبد عليه أولاً أن يحل عقدتا قديمه ويعقدها مرا أخرى (كما في حال في الدين

(Shamaism))

ثمانية طلاباً لتحقيق المال أو الامنيات، طاوس ملك كبير الملائكة عند اليزيدية الدين جهله نصوصهم الدينية في كتابهم الدينية لقد فقدتى في عدده قرون الديانة اليزيدية تعتمد وجود كتاب المقدس يسمى مصحف رش وأماء الكتاب المنزل وهذه التسميه الذي تسميه أيضا في كتاب مردهوس أو أي هرله ... (الشمس)) العين البيضاء يطلقون علي ... نظام تقع أسفل المعبد داخل الكهف كبير عندما كل شخص يدخل بئر الزمزم (أي بدين أصبح حبي أي حاج بئر الزمزم وعندما تجرح من كهف بواحد باب يؤدي الى عرفة دفن فيها محمد الديانة اليزيدية والرجل أهمها في تاريخها شيخ عادى ما فكارى هذا هو ولمن حافظ درجة الثالثه في تجمع اليزيدى هو من حافظ على أمن كثير من طقوس وعبادات المدرسة التي كادت أن ينفرض المجتمع اليزيدى ينالف من طبقات وفق نظام ترابط عامودى وتتألف تابع من ثلاثة درجات هي الشيخ والبير والمريد، الديانه اليزيديه معناها هذه الطبقه (الطبقه) مثل ما موجود في طريقة القشريه أي في ماص المجتمع وأنها هي نظام طبقي ديني هذه الديانه ليست تشيرا بل لابد أن يعتنق أن يكون اليزيديا في الولادة ومن يتجر أن خروج من مراجعهم من عوده اليها وهو ما قلص أعداد اليزدين كثيرين خلال عقود خرنا بسب أصطهاد باقي الديانات الباقي لهم من قديم الزمان هذه الديانة مغلقه لاينقل واحد أن يأتي لان أن يدخل لأي مكله لا ينقل أن يرجع اليها في مصر راهبان مؤلان عن طقوس هو يابا شاويس وبير وكلهم موضوعان من الزواج ويسميهم المردين بارك في اشاره الى الحياه في هذه المعبد في تعليم المناسك وعبادات اليزيديه وتبعد في أعلى

-٢-   العراق معقل للديانة الأيزيدية

من مكان بعيد لإطلالة المدون ويحيط به جباله وجمالته الأيزيدية في قلب
مدينة لشنغان إلى بوسط ثقافة بين الدهوك والموصل كانت
دراسة لرحلة إلى وادي لالش كالمكان المقدس لطقوس الديانة الأيزيدية
التي بعد دورة كشف حقائقها غير وادي طويل رحلنا إلى عالم كم حافظة
كنيسة على أربقرون والأيزيديين الديانات القديمة وتعود أقدم الديانات في
وادي لالش ويتجاوز عمرها إلى خمسة آلاف سنة وتقوم كما يقولون على
تقديس الإنسان لظواهر الطبيعة ولا نعرف بوجود إله بين
الإنسان والإله؟ حيث منطقة محرمة في منطقة ما توطوها أقدم والغرباء
يجب أن تكون من أقدم لحامه سافة ما تتجاوز 30 مترا مقدسا لالش المق
إلى بنايات القديمة على حانب هذا الطريق ثم مائي أول عطاء وواحة الزائرة
التطهر ((أوتعميد)) تبدأ زيارة من العمق السماء التي يتم منها الأطفال وكل
الأيزيدية نور معبد لالش حيث تتولى المرمت السيده
كبير ؟ من لن تقسم أرفع من لنا بين بساء المعبد كما قالت المرأة لابد أن يحضر
كل الأيزيدي إلى السر التعميد لحصول على البركة هذا أمر واجب وإلا ما شرنا
بتر دينه ولا تقبل ديانته كما قال الديانه لأيزيده متنطبه في الله مباشرا
لا يوجد في ديانه الأيزيديه أي ذكر من الأنبياء في عبادهم بل يوجد من
المتطرفين ؟؛ أن المعبد يوثق تاريخ المعبد الذي يقول لرجال الدين الأيزيدون
من بنيته (هذا الباب) سطوفان نبي نوح Noah وعلى جره اليمين نفس
بابه بارزة أفعى السوداء (يحرم الديانة لأيزيديه قتل) لم يبكنه بأنها وجسده من أرواح الحياة
كما قال الحيه السوداء وإذا لا تكون أذى على أهل لذلك يمع من قتلها أنه مقدسه ولا
بقتلها ولا تبكوا الذي في الحياه السوداء يعم مشاركة شيء ثاني كما يعتقدون
يوجد دلائل لحياه وإذا إنقذت سفينة نوح (هذا لم تكن ولا كانت *
مدونة في (عهد القديم) كما يدعون هذا . عبدة المعبد لا يصلى أين تلك أقدام
البس كما يوحدني إلى أبي المعبد النبه داود نجمه داود
وبيت النعمه داود ٭ حيه سوداء ✡ ماء ← مدخل
الرهان مكتوبه أخيرذلك حيه كما يدعون
٭ هذه دلائل ليست مدونه في كتاب مقدس   ثم
من التوراه وعهد القديم لم يذكر ذلك النبي صدقهم وأنا كتب الله كم أدينكم أوصركم لتعميد

تكمله بكتاشي -- ب --

الآسيا الصغرى صين ويابان وأمريكا. الباشا في نقطه أنطلاق

(الدين البكتاشيه) ويريدون من طرف الدرويس نريد أن حصول لنا على اعتراف

بنا وقوم جديا كالطائفه الدينيه مستقله بما يظهر اليوم البكتاشيه المراسله

الصوفيه الاسلاميه منتشره في أسس بين المتصوفة نفقان وبقى الروحي

في البلبان في مركز العالمى البكتاشيه تناح الى الولا القائد الروحي والشيخ

الطريق وهو اليوم السر أبن برهمال ومعروف في الخارج بالمبنى

كل شيء الباني كل شيء مستقل ولم بندو أم جديدا أو تاريخنا وحفر اعنه مع

علم الاسلام لكن في هل هذه حقيقه أمن وهو مرع س الاسلام ؟ وبتطور

مع تطور مع الزمن البكتاشيه هي طريقه الصوفية ذات عقيده الباطنيه

علم هو دين برسي كما عندهم الأركان الخمسه الاسلاميه وأرساطهم في عقيدة

القلوبن والخ البكتاشيه نفس الواجبات مشتركه مع المسلمى

الشهاد م ٢- الصلاة ٣- الصيام ٤- والزكاء و الخ لذلك البكاشيه

لريانفى الواجبات عموم المسلمى أصانته ذلك كائن في مرانت

الدريسه يسعى مؤمنى سرعلم في وصول الى جوهر الايمان وهي شريعه

والطريقه والمعروه والحقيقه البكتاشيه طريقه علينا عابره الى حدود

ليست اليانيه صعبا أن رفها في الباشا الاناشأ أما تعود الى القرن

ثالث عشر وكان ذلك في بلاد الأصول حيث تأسله أول بكته

على يد الحاج دكتاش الوليد وأمه المسد محمد أبراهيم وبخنوا نفقدنا ل

رسول وديسه يعود الى الامام الموسى الفاض وهو مرس الأول لطريقه

الصوفيه البكتاشيه وهي تسير على دينا كحسب اصله التركماني ولكن

عاشه في بلاد الفارس ومن ثم رجع الى تركيا*

* ٹ * * ٹ
* * * ن ب *
ٹ * * ٹ *
* ٹ ب
* ٹ *
* ٹ

-٢-

البكتاشي

ولده في عائلة بكتاشيه البانيه وهي ولم تكن متدينه في صيفه الحال

كل أصحاب الديانات في البانيا الشيوعيه التي كانت تحارب تدين بكل

أشكاله وتمنع ممارسته وكل أشكاله بعد أنتهاء الشيوعيه والدكتاتوريه

تنفس البلاد من الحريه جيدا جيدا رجع الدين وأصبح أصحابه يمارسون

الطقوس هذا على الأول الكبار وأما الصغار فكان عليهم أن يبدؤا تعلم من

جديد من من أراد كذلك وكانت العائله والأقارب أولا وأول مصدر لتعلم

ومن التأكيد وأنهم يقنعون أبناء بأن دينهم أو مذهبهم هو الحق ورأى أن غيره

هو الباطل مهما شيء طبيعي على اختلاف الأديان المعتقدات لكن هذه

الطريقه في التعلم تخلط التاريخ في الخرافات والحقائق في الهوان خاصه الذي

يتعلق من الأقليات كما هو حال في طائفه البكتاشيه البكتاشيه كما رأها

في وضع الخاص سوى في داخل الالبانيه أم عموم المسلمين في العالم مهناك

يعتبرونها المذهب الحقيقي داخل الحد الاسلامي وهناك الاخرون

يعتبرون قدجاءه عن طريق الحكوم يروهن بعيده عن اللسنى والمبادي

الاسلام بينا كثر جيران الاوربي يعبرونها أسلاما وبعد ذلك يتعامل معها

كالاسلام في عالم أوربي والمسيحي المحيط أمحسى سلمان يعرفون

جميع والبكتاشي ليس أسماء بل البكتاشي نظرا للأبن من أتباع طريقه

البكتاشيه يسعى الى طريقه دخله البكتاشيه من بدايتها وأبناء علوم يعلمني

أن أتصل على أجابات شافيه وتسورات الواضحه على تلك اشكاليات

أعلم من هذه رحلتي تشبه كثير من الغام بحث عن طريقه دينسه يعني من

يعتبرها هي من هه سماء أخرين يعبرونها رشدا من عمل الشطان وكيانا هذا

وذلك يموت (بتيله) أمرا واقع لا أريد من هذه رحلتي أكبر على حقيقه هذا

المذهب أو غير فقط أريد التوسع في دراسه والتعمق في تاريخ وأصول أشياء قراءه

من مصدر على أفكار وآراء كهميات منطقه من داخل المذهب نفسه وخارجيه

ومن أخرهم الملايين بتركي بتوجد البكتاشي في منطقه البلقان فأضافه الى

البانيا بتواجدون فكل من مقدونيا ودوبان وكوزوفو وجبل الاسود

وبوسنيا ومجر وبلغاريا ورومانيا وهناك البكتاشيه فكل من

<u>تركيا وأيران وعراق وسوريا ولبنان ومصر</u> الى جانب تواجدهم من جمهوريات

الديانة الكاكائية في العراق
((الياراسانية)) ملك   وأما أحترمكونهم يؤمنون في الله.

يصومون ثلاثه أيام ويرفضون تعدد الزوجات ويبيحون ملك خير إلا أذا يريدون
معلم مسلمين ، مالا نعرفه على طائفه الكاكائية في العراق يعيشون في العراق
وأيران وتركيا وأوسط أسيا منذ الألف السنين وحتى قبل ظهور ديانات
الألهوريه في العراق أغلب يعيشون في كردستان وينتمون إلى عرقيه الكرد
ويعود تاريخهم إلى ثلاثه الألاف قبل الميلاد ويبجح في حب كلامهم هو
جميعهم كما يابو أحد في عقيدتهم يحلون بدرجه الأنبياء كان أحدهم
السلطان أسحاق الذي يعتبر بيثا بنبه النبي أو المرجع الدين لديانة الكاكائية
ويؤمنوا الكاكائيون بوجود خالق الواحد ولديهم الطقوس والعبادة خاصتنا
بهم منها الصوم والصلاة وصرورت أن يتحلى أتباع الديانة في طهارة والصدق
والتواضع والقناعة والصوم عندهم هو أمتناع عن الطعام وأكثر من ثلاثه أيام
خلال النهار ومن ثم يحتفلون بعدها في العيد ليوم الواحد ونفصل ذلك
في أيام الخميس خلال فصل الشتاء، أما صلاتهم عندهم هي عبارة عن
أدعيه والمنوياحات مناجاة تقوم بها في الفجر والمغرب وطقوس
عباده الأخرى لديهم تتمثل في الاجتماعات الدينيه تعقد مرة واحده
شهريا بتعويض عن كل ما كاكائيه تقدم نذرا خلال هذه الاجتماعات وهذا
نذر يتمثل بتقديم الفوكه أو أي نوع أخر من الطعام، يحمل أعضاء أجتماع
الدعاء (دعاء) والمناجاة كما يسمو الكاكيون، تعدد الزوجات حتى لو لم
يكن تجب ويتنشأ من ذلك حالات بعذر بها الرجل ما معه زوجته والمرأة
(أمرأه) لديهم مكانة مميزا متساويه في الحقوق والواجبات وحتى في الميراث
أنهم يمنعون طلاقهم إلا حالات نادره وفي أيضا المجرمين في حالات
الخيانة ومن عوده كلمة الكاكائيه فهو مصطلح يستخدم في العراق فقط
والتسميه الرسميه لديانه هي الياراسانيه ومعناها على الخالق وفي
دول الأخرى أبن مثل يطلقوا على أنواع هذه والديانة أصحاب الحق حتى يطلقوا
في أفغانستان وباكستان بتركيا وفي الرسال بستيه وفي تركيا هلوبن
وعن لفظ الكاكائيه هي مشتق من كلمه كاكا في اللغه الكردية وتعني أخي
الكبير أو المعرف   أنا بورى الأديان السماويه   أحترم

في وجود أهميه كلم يؤمنون
الأديان أحترم الأديان
أمنى وجود الله

□ * ؟ * ٤
△ * ✝ * ج
╬ * ⊞ * ⊞

من هم الشبك ؟

من هم الشبك ؟ الديانه القوميه أو الطائفه ؟!

أحقيقه الشبك الأقوام عاشوا في سهل نينوى من منطقة نور ان وحتى الخلب، والشبك ناس مسالميين ويحترمون الجيران، وأما مستقرتهم هم سونه (سُنّه) وشيعه ولكن أكثر الشبك هم من طائفه الشيعه الأماميه وتقريباً الشبك هم أخواننا الشّنّه (شيعه) المذاهب الأربعه هنا بسألني العراق في أشكال والمكونات شنو (ماهو) مكون الشبك عن عبرولي سيد المكون الشبكي هو جزء منهم وهؤلاء الشبك ما موجودين في المكان من العالم إلا في العراق وتقاليدهم في تنوع الديني موجودين في عراق فقط ولهم (لهم) لغة تميزهم عن أعرهم اللغة الشبكيه لغة جاصه بيهم اللغه التي تجمعهم تتكون من عدده (عدد) اللهجات يعني بيها الكلمات أو يعني الكلمات العربيه بها (فيها) الكلمات تركمه وبها كلمات الفارسيه فيها كلمات الكرديه يعني (تعني) مزج الشبك يتكلمون اللغه العربيه العربيه ومع بعضهم يتكلمون اللغه الشبكيه كما دُونه كلمات مختلفه من عدد اللغات! الشبك مشهورين في زراعه الزيتون والخضره في بدايه الخمسينات صارت أو أصبحت الهجره من الريف إلى المدينه بغيه الحصول عن العمل في الموصل مع تأسس المصانع وتقدم مكنه في العراق كثير من الشبك أنتقلوا من القريه إلى المدينه ولكن بعد (٢٠٠٣) (2003) دخول القاعده إلى الموصل أضطروا الجوء العكسيه رجعوا إلى من هم سبب ما قتلوا منهم أعداد الكبيره على يد قاعده؟ أكثر القرايا (القرى) أكثر السنه وشيعي؟ الشبك أنتشروا في محافظات العراق بعد أنتشار الشبكي في محافظات العراق تأثروا في التقاليد الواقعه الثقافيه وقرأوا الكتب الثقافيه؟ الآن عندهم علم شبكي وأذاعه الشبكيه والشعار وهناك المؤلفات في العمل الآخر الذي صار الذي صار غير العامل الثقافي هو أنتشار الفكر في مجتمع الشبكي يعني (ماهو) سابقاً شبكي انقاعت موجودين في سهل نينوى فقط إلى محافظات الواقعه معهم لم يرجعوا إلى أراصيهم الدولي، فهرا يعني بعد مرور 100 سنه الشبك

الراهب (حباب)

Dec . 2022

من أقوى التقارير عن جامع براثا (أم سرياني) الاشرح في بغداد الجزء
الأول Albaghdadion - 66 k View . 7 mo ago . السعرا ديون

من أقدم بقعه في بغداد في منطقه القطيعه وتضم في منطقه القطيعه جامع براثا
جامع براثا من أقدم جوامع في العراق وكان في أساس كنيسه أو الدير
وصار جامع أو مسجد أثناء الخليفه عندما جاء الخليفه علي بن أبي طالب
إلى العراق وكان حربه في معركه النهروان بعد خروا رجع أبي طالب
(علي) من مكان الدير وسميه كنيسه براثا وبعدها سميه الجامع الراثا وكان
مسؤل عن الدير راهب هواسمه براثا وبقى هنا ثلاثه أيام وكان راهب
يعني يعرف أنه سيزوره بني أو الشخص وتم كما يقولون رجل براثا
(أمه حباب) وكان هذه كنسه قريبه إلى بغداد المدوره . قريب
أو مكان مقابر القريش الكاظميه نسبه سعر عبد الحسن كاظم قريه من
في داخل المسجد يوجد صخره سوء كما يقال مكان السيدنا ويسمى صفحه مريم
العذراء عليه . في منطقه من منطقه يسمى براثا أو صويانا وتسمى
أيضا القتمقه أو نبذه على مسجد براثا بعد مسجد الراثا أو ساجدوا أثار القديمه
قبل قد وجده بغداد القديمه (المدوره) عن هذا المكان سنه ۲۸٤ ۳۸ هجريه قبل بنى
مدينه بغداد في قبل بناء بغداد في ۱۰۸ سنوات ۱٤۰ سنه بنت بناء بغداد
في سنه ۱٤٥ سنه في زمن أبو جعفر المنصور . عندما عاد علي بن أبي طالب من
معركه نهروان وكان معه مشاء ألف مقاتل هذا كان عدد كبير جدا عندما نزل علي
كان راهب يتعبد في صومعه ويتعبد لله وهو بيت من نصارى أي به الحالديا أو
الكلدايا. صومعه زار راهب أعزه له صومعه وعندما تقابل راهب على وقال راهب
من هو الرجل وقال له الراهب هل أنت نبي وثم قال له على لا وقال له بني قدمات
وعندما قال لي على لماذا اخفى البير البين فقال له حسنا ولكن الماوسال ثم قال على احفر
هنا مكان البير البئر وحفروا ووجدوا صخره سوداء ولم يستطيع قلعوا ولكن على
دفعها (علي) . ثم عين البير وضفت يم العذراء أبنها مسيح عليها على صخره بيضاء
الذي وجدوها في البير على براثا كأنه متكونة من مقطوعه من (أذن) وأنا
أرض عباس الارض عباس، والصويانا أو آرامية، القديمة القتمقه أو منطقه
منطقه . وكانت في هذه المنطقه سوق النصارى أو الكاثير في أنت تسمى
قريه سونيا . ثم جلعوا المسلمين في هذه منطقه وغنموا بعض الغنائم (خالد بن وا)

الديانة المزدكيه

الديانة المزدكيه : الإباحى : الديانى : خطيئته : sin : المعاصى : عصيانا

الديانة المزدكيه : وأباحت الأموال وحقتها للناس شركه فيه

الديانة المزدكيه من أعنف الديانات فى التاريخ أباحها وهم كل قيم الديانه
مزدك وهى من الفوضويه ومنسأها الفنيه الجنسيه الاشتراكيه على الأموال
والزوجين والأعراض (الفرص) وتمتح حتى تنبى والأخوات (أحت) أى
رغم أن الديانه قديمه لكن عن قوة عبرها تطبق أغلب الدول الفرنسيه أى
حكاية الديانه فى الضبط وماهى حياتها بجوار هو فارس أسبه مزدك

لقد ولد فى بلاد الفارسى ميلاد دوله بين ٤٦٧م بين ٤٦٧ معروف فى
٤٨٧، ٤٩٧م، ٤٦٧
A.C
ميلادى ولكن بتقولوا البعض أن الديانه المزدك (المزدكيه وأنا أصول الديانه أنبره
المزدكيه ترجع قبل المزدك فى كتير لكن هو جدول لها كانت الديانه أنبره
أنبره فى أبران وهى الديانه الزردشتيه معروف أتباعها المجوس
وهى لو عبدة النار كالمجوس وهم يعبون إله واحد (أهورا) زدشته بتلك
القوة واحدة (هو اله) ولكنهم يشاركوا مع إله الأخرى مثل
الديان الوشيه من يسله بعض المؤرخى والناس حتى أن الديانه
الزردشتيه ديانه من أتباعه فى أبان لكن قد حرفوا أتباعها عن الدين
وأركوكوا إله يوحد تشابه بنا المزدكشته
المزدكيه حركه مماهصته إلى الزردشته وأنوا
الذى عند المجوس هو أغورى مزدى بدأ مزدى فى التبشير
فى ديانته جديده أن الناس سواء (سواء) وأن المال ل وأن أنا
ناس لا يعرفو بضمم بأن اله هو اله الذى هلوا ولا اله وأنا أودن
الضرورى وأت وأثر ضرورى فأحل كل نساء والرجال ووضع
ناس شى بى وقد أنتشرت حياه المزدكه بين شبان وأغنياء
كان باجه نمها وأسهامك الفاسمك قعبات الاول وأعت الدول وأوضى
الأخلاقفه وطفان الشهون والتنوذ إلى جراللن كبى أنوشروان
رجع الديانة للديانه الزدشتيه وأنشتم البه من طقوس المزدكه وبلد فارس وبلد
معاوضوا على أعياد المكانى وحزنى ديانه شياطيسك عند مى الأسلام فى أيران
فى ليالى أعياد والنكاتن وهم توجدمنها إلى قبل يارنونا خفيه دين أحى وشكرا

مقدمه

السلام عليكم ورحمه الله وبركاته يا أخواتي وأخواني الأعزاء وأبناء من الصفحه الثري ومن خط يدي أبدأ كتابتي وتدويني في هذا كتابي = Book "2" =

* (ظهور أول الأديان والعقائد والمذاهب والأيمان)
الأرضي منذو ظهور أول حضارات في وادي الرافدين Mesopotamia وفي كل بقاء أجزاء العالم، حيث بدأة من التدوين بعض الكلمات وكتابته في هذا كتاب أكتابي التي تحتوي علي عبارات وظهور أول عبادات، وتقدس علي النص حيث مرة عنها في أكتب مرت في تأليف هذا الكتاب والكتب الأخري مثل كتاب

What the Names in the Bible mean وكتاب Weeds

Weeds و أسوء Weed part 2 وكذلك

وكتاب أخر جزء ثاني

Notice Book Early Short History of the first of Civilization of Mankind on Earth

((Daneal))

أمين * المبين وكاتب والمؤلف هذا الكتاب : جورج أرشو...

J.E.B.

مقدمه -

السلام عليكم ورحمة الله وبركاته يا أخواتي وأخواني

الأعزاء وأبناء من الصنف البشري / ومن خط يدي

أبدأ كتابتي وتدوين من هذا كتابي ⟵ = 2 Book

* (ظهور أول الأديان والعقائد والمذاهب) والأديان

الأرض منذ ظهور أول حضارات في وادي الرافدين

Mesopotamia وفي كل بقاء أنحاء العالم، حيث بدأة من التدوين بعض

الكلمات وكتابته في هذا كتاب / كتابي التي تحتوي على عبادات

وأول ظهور أول عبادات وتقديس على النص حيث مرأة عمها في الكتب

التي أحضرها في مكتباتي / البيبسي وسمعت عنها حيث وأنا بدوري

مررت في تأليف هذا الكتاب والكتب الأخرى مثل كتاب

Weeds وكتاب What the Names in the Bible mean جزء ثاني

وWeeds و ألبوم Weed part 2 وكذلك

Notice Book Early Short History of the first of Civilization of
Mankind on Earth

وفي سوف أكتفي في تدوين والأرض الله سكان وتعالى إذا أبقائنا

أحياء سالمين إنشاء الله أدعوني ربي العالمين أن يبقي أحياء وحيات

طويلة مليئة من رحمته وحبه سلمه والأحياء وأحياكم جميعاً أمين

أخواتي والأخواني في تدوين في هذا كتابي أني لا أعارض الأضد أحد

وأي أفكاركم من أي بين الشرهما كانت هو شر ومن ضد أحد ودنيا

وأنا لست أمي لأسأل والأضت عضا القاصي القوي هو الله + أمين

منكم بين اثنين وأمين (جوزيف أو سوف) أي أضيب دائماً وأنا

أضب أعمال والحسنه إلى أقدتير وتعليم من الكتب السماويه هي

بني أدم وأحكامكم مقدر وقد أراوحيت دونها أنا وأنا بدوري لا أعارض في أي

معكم وأحبكم أنكم أخواتي وأخواني / وحين وقصة من هذا الكتاب وفي خط وكتابه

تدويني / وأنا بدوري أقول لكم أخواتي أني شر مثلي أنا شر أفوق بين وينسلك بقد أدي

مواليد وفي في الجيه والأمريكيه أنا خون في هذه الجنسيات ركز: جوزيف أبشو وي

(Daneal))

أمين * المسيح وكاتب والمؤلف هذا الكتاب: جوزيف أبشو وي

J.E.B.

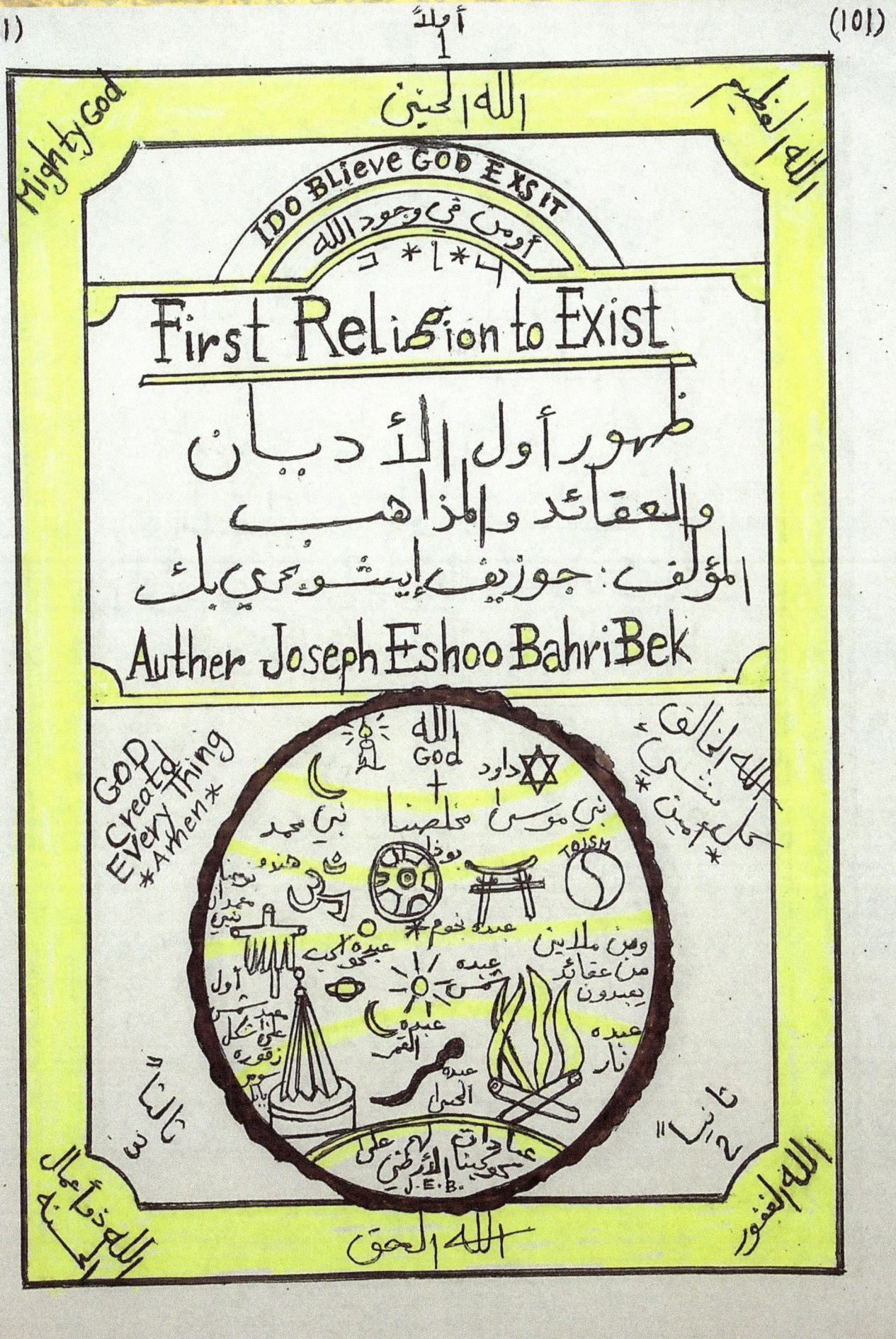

الله الحين

Mighty God

I DO BLieve GOD EXSIT

أومن في وجود الله

First Religion to Exist

ظهور أول الأديان
والعقائد والمذاهب
المؤلف: جوزيف إيشو بحري بك

Auther Joseph Eshoo Bahri Bek

GOD
Created
Every Thing
Amen

God
داود

TOISM

الله الحق

First Religion to Exist

Auther Joseph Eshoo Bahri Bek

IDO BLieve GOD EXSIT

Mighty God

GOD Createtd Every Thing * Amem *

TOISM

God